A BOUNDLESS FEAR GRIPPED ME

A BOUNDLESS FEAR GRIPPED ME

How the Other Half Lived in the Pandemic's Shadow

Documentation by
Pamela Philipose

Curation by
Anjali Bhardwaj and Amrita Johri

YODA PRESS
79 Gulmohar Enclave
New Delhi 110 049
www.yodapress.co.in

ISBN 978-93-82579-88-5

Editors in charge: Neha Madhusudan and Arpita Das
Typeset in Adobe Garamond Pro, 11/14.4, by MSourcing
Published by Arpita Das for YODA PRESS

Table of Contents

Foreword

We hope this book sparks discussion...

Damyanty Sridharan and Jyoti Rawal

The COVID-19 pandemic has affected each and every one of us in some way or the other. However, it is difficult to comprehend the impact it has had on the marginalised, and indeed the further deprived women, men, children due to precarity of work and exclusion based on gender identities. The essays in this volume give an indication of the multi-layered and multi-dimensional nature of the challenges faced by the marginalised: be it the homeless, unemployed, aged, differently-abled, or new-born infants living in the bastis of Delhi. Many exceptional reports published in the past, like *Towards Equality: The Report of the Committee on the Status of Women in India* (1974), and *Shramshakti: A Summary of the Report of the National Commission on Self-Employed Women and Women in the Informal Sector* (1988), as well as the *Report on Conditions of Work and Promotion of Livelihoods in the Unorganised Sector* (2007) produced by the National Commission for Enterprises in the Unorganised Sector, have brought out the distinct economic and social value of the so-called unorganised sector. While the crisis of the pandemic swept through India from March 2020, the uncertain nature of informal work led to much tangible and intangible loss. It became apparent how the absence of institutionalised universal social security responses, including food security, were among the major reasons for India seeing many reversals of the gains it had made in the social and economic sectors over the years.

The narratives in this book document the grim ground realities of Delhi's bastis during the pandemic. They make visible the humanitarian crisis of the pandemic by highlighting issues of violence against women, precarity of work, bottlenecks in education and health, and more. Each chapter attempts to bring to the reader the situations on the ground through the voices of those who have been directly impacted. Their words often express their traumas and tribulations, but they also convey words of hope and courage that speak of the will to change destinies. The questions raised by these stories point to the multi-layered reality of the poor and marginalised, that needs a similarly variegated and layered response from policy makers and other stakeholders, including employers, consumers, civic and civil society organisations.

Data, both quantitative and qualitative, informs action and policy. In this volume, Dipa Sinha, a leading academic, chalks out the existing aggregate health, livelihood, and social security situation of those at the margins. As she concludes, "The need for comprehensive, accessible and universal social protection extending to health, education and livelihood is unfortunately not yet evident in the political discourse of the city." Pamela Philipose validates this through the poignant realities she presents based on her interactions with the affected population. The prologue written by Anjali Bhardwaj and Amrita Johri reflect their close involvement in making visible the pandemic scenario. Both have been instrumental in mitigating the situation through advocacy, legal interventions and direct measures relating to food and livelihood security. Hopefully, the documentation of challenges and, in some cases, coping mechanisms of the marginalised in this volume will lead to a change in approach, birth a new willingness, and a framework to deal with the current and future crises. Ultimately, the book will serve its purpose if it leads to fruitful discussions on ensuring the security of food and livelihoods for all.

The work of the Friedrich Ebert Stiftung (FES) is centred on social democratic values of peace, solidarity and social justice. Within the overall gender approach, the Women's Empowerment and Gender Equality Project of FES India aims at the economic and political empowerment of women. Facilitating workshops, round tables and action-based research is an integral part of this work. We see this publication fulfilling just such a role and hope that it leads to policy initiatives in sync with the ground realities portrayed here.

The idea to conduct this documentation came from Sridharan and Rawal of the Friedrich Ebert Stiftung.

Prologue

A Humanitarian Crisis Like No Other

Anjali Bhardwaj and Amrita Johri

The COVID-19 crisis has revealed deep fault lines in our development paradigm. The pandemic has been likened to an X-ray that has exposed the bare bones of our system and amplified the terrible inequalities it has perpetuated.

According to government estimates, around 42 crore people work in the unorganised sector in the country, of which more than 10 crore are inter-state migrant workers. Often, the most marginalised from villages migrate to cities in search of livelihoods. Nearly 70 per cent of Delhi's population lives in unplanned settlements, including slums, and has systematically been made invisible. Hidden in shanty towns and bastis located in stretches adjoining highrise building complexes and plush colonies, the poor live bereft of basic infrastructure and services. The lifelines of the city's economy—working as construction labour, domestic help, drivers, security guards, plumbers, electricians, rickshaw pullers and hawkers—struggle to earn a minimum wage. Most are left out of the porous social security net, as they do not possess the requisite documents to apply for government programmes and schemes. Despite the exclusions and injustices, they work resiliently to sustain themselves with dignity.

The lockdowns imposed to combat the COVID-19 pandemic and the health crisis faced by millions in the second wave pushed the working poor over the brink. Lockdowns resulted in the instant cessation of all income-generating opportunities, hurling families into abject destitution. The little savings they did have ran out in no time, leaving them unable to afford even two square meals a day. Reassurances by the Prime Minister of India, and the Chief Minister of Delhi, that essential commodities will continue to be available in neighbourhood shops during lockdowns meant little to those who had no money. Forced to queue up for hours to get a meagre cooked meal, they endured indignity and had hunger thrust upon them. Lack of social infrastructure in the city, coupled with recurring expenses—the average rent for a *jhuggi* (dwelling) in Delhi is around Rs 3000—made it unviable for many to continue living in the city without any proper source of income. Heart-wrenching images of families carrying their young on their backs, walking towards villages hundreds of miles away, bore testimony to their economic fragility.

The severe food insecurity faced by people during the pandemic was no coincidence. It was the result of deliberate policy blindness. A very large percentage of the economically vulnerable are left out of the ambit of the food security net—the Public Distribution System—as the coverage under the National Food Security Act (NFSA) is not universal. Only 37 per cent of the 1.9 crore people living in Delhi are covered under the NFSA, which guarantees every beneficiary 5 kilos of foodgrain at subsidised rates every month.

Ration cards are only provided to those with a household annual income of less than Rs 1,00,000 and who are able to furnish Aadhaar cards, address proof and the electricity bill of their place of residence. The poorest and most marginalised are often excluded due to their inability to furnish the numerous documents required to apply for a ration card. The pandemic also underlined the problem associated with using income as a criterion for inclusion. Families of unorganised sector workers, who were managing to earn more than Rs 1,00,000 annually by working as drivers, construction workers, or household help before the pandemic, suddenly found themselves slipping below the poverty line, exposing the highly volatile nature of poverty in urban areas.

At a time when the Public Distribution System became a lifeline for the economically vulnerable, those who did not possess a ration card were pushed to the brink of hunger, even starvation. The extent of the problem was reflected in the fact that when the Delhi government started the initiative of providing temporary e-coupons to families without ration cards subsequent to an order of the High Court, it was found that in a city where 72 lakh people are ration card holders according to the government's own data, e-coupons were issued to only 70 lakh people.

The economic hardship was further exacerbated during the deadly second wave of COVID-19 in 2021, when afflicted families ran up huge debts while procuring essential drugs and oxygen cylinders from the black market in a bid to save their loved ones. Left with no means to pay rent for their dwellings, there were cases of people joining the ranks of the homeless in the city, squatting on roadsides, forced to beg for basic survival.

Even after the lockdowns were lifted, economic recession and fear of disease persisted, preventing resumption of employment for a vast majority. The pandemic had fallen like a rock wrecking the lives of the working poor who, in the true spirit of *atmanirbharta* (self-reliance), had created their fragile ecosystem without state support. The lives they had built for themselves were destroyed by biased policies that served to protect the haves—those who could afford "social distancing" and work from the comfort of their well-appointed homes. The poor were left to deal with hunger, destitution, and mounting debt.

Satark Nagrik Sangathan (SNS) and other constituent members of the Delhi Rozi Roti Adhikar Abhiyan (DRRAA), who have been working with residents of slum settlements for many decades, organised "Hunger Hearings"—public hearings on food and social insecurity—in a bid to highlight the destitution and hardships faced by people. The heart-rending testimonies of those who shared their experiences highlighted the urgent need to document the humanitarian crisis that unfolded in the city. The idea to produce this book, capturing the tribulations of the urban poor during the COVID-19 pandemic in Delhi, was thus born.

Senior journalist Pamela Philipose has been closely associated with struggles of the working poor and has a deep understanding of issues of food and social insecurity faced by them. She spent significant time meeting those who have suffered deeply—single women and widows who were forced to travel back to their villages with their children during the lockdowns, only to return as there was no means of sustenance even there; families that lost loved ones and fell into debt traps; those rendered homeless due to the pandemic; children forced to drop out of school and seek work to support hapless relatives. She captured their challenges and pain, the coping strategies they adopted and, most importantly, their stories of struggle and resilience. This book will serve as a historical record of the impact of one of the most devastating humanitarian crises on Delhi's unorganised sector workers and their families.

Introduction

Delhi's Precarious Citizens

Dipa Sinha

Delhi is not only the capital city of India, but also its richest. The Global Metro Monitor, 2018, of the Brookings Institute ranks Delhi sixth among the 300 largest metro area cities in the world in terms of the Economic Performance Index. The city also remains the destination of choice for thousands of migrant workers from nearby states for its promise of economic opportunities; it also attracts the second highest number of inter-state migrants, following Mumbai. According to Census 2011, 42 per cent of the city's population reported themselves as migrants. Delhi is not only a melting pot of cultures, languages and classes but also a microcosm of all of India's contradictions. Inequality is high and visible. While almost half the city's population lives in the slums, it also has a large homeless population.

Even before the COVID-19 pandemic, Delhi was known to be a tough place to survive in, especially for those with meagre resources. There are major shortcomings in terms of infrastructure with access to basic services; housing, drinking water, and sanitation are a challenge for most. Delhi also faces the highest crime rates amongst Indian cities with appallingly high levels of violence against women. About 70 per cent of the workforce is in the unorganised sector, working jobs with neither security of contract nor any social protection. Although better than the national average, the levels of malnutrition in Delhi are still high. According to the National Family Health Survey (NFHS-4), 32 per cent of children under 5 years of age in the city are stunted, and more than half the women and young children are anaemic.

The pandemic, along with its accompanying lockdowns, has exposed these fault lines clearly. While everyone's lives were disrupted in one way or the other by it, the poor have been disproportionately affected as seen in the various experiences documented in this book.

The Health Crisis

Delhi is one of the cities that has been most affected by the pandemic. The first wave witnessed a peak of about 10,000 new COVID-positive cases a day by October 2020, putting pressure on the healthcare system for both testing and treatment. The second wave was much worse, with a peak of more than 28,000 new cases in a day by April 2021. The entire healthcare system collapsed under the pressure of rising cases; there was an acute shortage of drugs, injectables, hospital beds, and even oxygen. There is no count of how many died due to lack of access to appropriate health care. Based on Civil Registration System (CRS) data, *The Hindu* estimated that 55,239 "excess deaths" were registered in Delhi ever since the COVID-19 pandemic hit (from April 2020 to June 2021), which is 2.2 times the official reported figure of 24,977 COVID-19 deaths for the same period. The undercount factor is even higher (3.4) were we to consider the period January–June 2021 solely, owing to the surge in mortality during the second wave. On a single day, on April 23, 46 deaths were reported in two hospitals in Delhi due to oxygen shortage.

The healthcare system was just not equipped to deal with the crisis at hand; this resulted in a chaotic situation where each individual patient had to fend for herself. While reports say that other cities such as Mumbai had centralised call centres (war rooms) that facilitated people's access to hospital care, in Delhi, during the second wave, it was up to patients to contact individual hospitals, one by one, in search of a bed. Citizens' collectives, volunteer helplines, gurudwaras, Resident Welfare Associations, all stepped in to do their bit. For those who had access, social media became another space to source information, drugs, hospital beds and more. However, it was extremely difficult, if not impossible, for the poorest of the population to even access such spaces (see Chapter 10). Additional facilities had been set up during the first wave but were shut down as soon as it ended. They were reopened during the second wave but only after the infection had peaked, and the system was completely overwhelmed. Based on this disastrous experience, the government made a number of arrangements to expand facilities. Nevertheless, there is still not enough attention being paid towards strengthening the healthcare system comprehensively.

India is amongst the lowest public spenders on health in the world. The available facilities are concentrated in urban and metropolitan areas. As a result, Delhi serves the tertiary care needs of a large number of people from the neighbouring states as well, because of the shortage of health facilities in those areas. Ensuring that Delhi's population has access to equitable and good quality health care also remains a challenge. While the Delhi government had initiated the Mohalla Clinics (neighbourhood clinics) which could contribute to improving access to primary health care, only 203 of them were functional towards the end of 2019, although the government had promised to open 1000 clinics. Data as of the end of December 2018, presented in a report by Praja.org, shows that compared to sanctioned positions, 21 per cent medical staff and 50 per cent paramedical staff positions in MCD-run dispensaries and hospitals remained vacant. High vacancies were seen in state-run hospitals and dispensaries as well, with 34 per cent medical staff and 29 per cent paramedical staff positions being vacant. A survey conducted by them in 2019 further found that only 6 per cent of Delhi's population had some form of health insurance and residents in Delhi spent 9.8 per cent of their annual income on health expenses. With the pandemic, this poor healthcare infrastructure was obviously under stress, as people's healthcare expenditures rose even higher.

Issues of access to health care are also compounded by the unique nature of the governance structure in the city, with parallel structures run by the central government, the state government and the municipal corporations. This became evident during the second wave, when conflicting positions were taken by the central and state governments on issues such as availability of oxygen. These issues ultimately had to be mediated by judicial authorities. The larger problem was a disconnect between the state hospitals, central government hospitals and private providers, which made it more difficult for an average citizen to access even basic services.

Vulnerability and Loss of Livelihoods

The various case studies in this book show that the pandemic has not only resulted in a health crisis, but it has also caused many to grapple with homelessness, displacement, job loss, hunger, indebtedness, domestic violence, and loss of education for children. In fact, the economic crisis first started with the national lockdown, resulting in an exodus of migrant workers headed back to their villages. While no official records are available, thousands were forced to move out of the city in buses, and many more walked hundreds of kilometres to reach their homes. Informal workers, small business owners, and even students were forced to leave Delhi as they were bereft of any social support, and could not afford to stay back and pay exorbitant rents while not earning an income. In a few months, as things began to open up and people started coming back, the second wave once again enforced extended curfews and renewed uncertainty. It is estimated that about 1.3 million migrant workers left Delhi during the second wave of COVID-19.

The effects of the pandemic on Delhi's population need to be understood against the backdrop of economic and social inequality, poor quality of jobs, inadequate public infrastructure, especially for the poor, and a whole host of issues related to citizenship and sense of identity. Delhi's unemployment rate, at 10.4 per cent, is much higher than the national average of 5.8 per cent (according to estimates of the Periodic Labour Force Survey, 2019–20 conducted by the National Statistical Office, Government of India). According to a report of the Indian Social Science Trust (ISST) based on Periodic Labour Force Survey data, about 79 per cent of employed men and 73 per cent of employed women in Delhi earn their livelihood working in the informal sector. Most people therefore have no savings or assets that they can fall back on in times of crises such as the pandemic.

One of the issues that enhances the vulnerability of the working poor in the city is that of inadequate housing. A report by the Housing and Land Rights Network (HLRN), "In Search of a Home"—based on interviews with migrant workers from Delhi who had returned to their villages—found that most of the respondents did not have access to adequate housing in Delhi, with about 86 per cent of them living in rented rooms without any tenure security. Over 12 per cent of the respondents indicated that direct loss of housing was one of the main reasons for them leaving Delhi during the lockdown. 16 per cent said that they were harassed by the homeowners for rent. While Delhi's Chief Minister Arvind Kejriwal made an appeal to homeowners to not collect rent during the pandemic period, most reports suggest that without any alternate mechanism, this was an untenable proposition. For most homeowners in poorer localities, the rent is also a source of livelihood; moreover, there are no written rental agreements and their own property rights are often unclear. Additionally, there is also the issue of poor access to other public facilities. According to the National Family Health Survey-4, 20 per cent of Delhi's households do not have access to an improved drinking water source (making them dependent on tankers/public tubewells), and about 30 per cent of the households are not using an improved sanitation facility (resulting in open defecation). Furthermore, even during the pandemic, demolition drives continued to make people (like Sameena and Ruby, interviewed in Chapter 7) homeless.

The economic slowdown also had a gendered impact in many ways. Only about 16 per cent of women in Delhi participate in the labour force, and of them, most are in the informal sector. Of those counted as workers, almost one-third work as domestic workers and home-based workers (see Chapter 2). Women are also involved in construction work, street vending and so on. These are all areas that were disproportionately affected during lockdowns (as in the case of Putul, in Chapter 4, for instance). They are also sectors with little protection in the form of social security provisions or minimum wage enforcement. A number of studies show that while there has been some recovery in employment after the national lockdown in 2020, fewer women than men have been absorbed back in the labour force. Further, there are also reports of increased domestic violence because of the overall situation of crisis within households (as is the case with Sarika, in Chapter 5). Moreover, with most family members now spending more time at home and facilities such as schools and anganwadis which provided some support being closed, the burden of unpaid work on women has increased significantly.

A large number of the women employed by the government work as frontline workers—Accredited Social Health Assistants (ASHAs), an all-woman cadre of "voluntary" workers, and anganwadi workers. They are not recognised as "employees" and are paid an "honorarium" or "incentive", not a salary. Through the pandemic, anganwadi workers were involved in home delivery of rations for children, pregnant and lactating women. Furthermore, ASHA workers were mobilised to conduct surveys, awareness campaigns, and so on. These women earn around Rs 6000–7000 a month, and are given very little job protection. Despite working long hours under risky conditions, ASHA workers, who have been the backbone of the state's community-level response to the pandemic, face issues of low wages and often delayed payments. Throughout 2021, they have therefore organised a number of protests to raise their issues but have not had much response.

State Response

The devastating impact of the pandemic on people's lives was also exacerbated by the failure of the state to undertake mitigation measures. While the government did undertake a number of steps towards improving the situation and providing some social protection to the people, these were often late and insufficient. The health infrastructure was expanded temporarily, while no systemic measures were taken to improve overall health access in the city.

A number of short-term measures were undertaken to address hunger. Temporary community kitchens were set up in schools and homeless shelters across the city that provided free meals twice a day, although they were many more in number in 2020, compared to 2021. Free foodgrains and ration kits were made available through the Public Distribution System (PDS) under the central government's Pradhan Mantri Garib Kalyan Anna Yojana (PMG-KAY), and through additional state support. While this turned out to be a lifesaver for those who had a ration card, many without cards were excluded—only 37 per cent of Delhi's population have ration cards). Following pressure from civil society as well as the High Court, the Delhi government started an e-coupon scheme for those who did not have ration cards. Under this scheme, rations were given for two months; nearly 70 lakh coupons were issued in 2020. In 2021, the Delhi government distributed foodgrains (only once) to those who did not have ration cards, but with allocations for only 30 lakh people.

Groups such as the Delhi Rozi Roti Adhikar Abhiyan (DRRAA) monitored the distribution of food through these schemes and helped people access them. The public hearings organised by the DRRAA drew attention to the fact that while these additional interventions were very useful for those who managed to access them, there were many who were left out for various reasons. Further, these schemes were very short-term in nature, just a couple of months each time, thereby leaving the larger issue of food insecurity and malnutrition unaddressed.

A one-time cash assistance of Rs 5000 was also provided to auto and taxi drivers, and construction workers during both years. Under the Mukhyamantri COVID-19 Pariwar Aarthik Sahayata Yojana, an ex-gratia amount of Rs 50,000 was to go to every family that had lost a member to COVID-19 and an additional Rs 2500 per month if the deceased was the sole breadwinner of the family. For all such schemes, the barriers related to registration and documentation are not easy to cross (as seen in the case of Gautam Giri trying to get compensation for his mother Arti's death in Chapter 10).

Looking Ahead

While these are all limited, short-term responses, what is missing is a more equitable re-imagination of the city-state's development. The precarity of the informal workforce and the contested citizenship of the urban poor are well-known issues in India. However, the pandemic and the ensuing lockdowns have exposed the vulnerability of the millions of workers and their families in the urban informal sector in a manner that it can no longer be denied or hidden. Even as the pandemic recedes, we will take much longer to recover from the crises it leaves behind, unless some very serious measures are undertaken. In recognition of the human cost of the pandemic, what is urgently needed is a vision for rebuilding the city in an equitable and sensitive manner.

Moreover, irrespective of the pandemic, the events of the past two years have exposed the lack of social protection as well as decent employment opportunities for the majority of the population. The impact of the lockdowns and the pandemic are difficult to quantify immediately; even comprehending their nature in the short-run is hard. For example, the closure of schools and disruptions in access to education will have a long-term impact on lives and livelihoods in different ways. Similar is the case of healthcare and nutrition. The need for comprehensive, accessible and universal social protection extending to health, education, and livelihood is unfortunately not yet evident in the political discourse of the city.

Dipa Sinha teaches Economics at the School of Liberal Studies, Dr. B.R. Ambedkar University, Delhi. She is associated with the Right to Food Campaign.

Chapter 1

The Never-Ending Search for Sanctuary During the Pandemic

The documentation in this chapter and those that follow is based on detailed interactions with the residents of the bastis and homeless shelters of Delhi that took place in the months of July and August 2021. The punishing Delhi summer was at its height, the second wave of the pandemic—which had led 1.3 million to leave the city—had barely receded, and the traumas it had wrought were still apparent on the faces of the women, men, and children I interviewed. Assisting me in these conversations was Satark Nagrik Sangathan's representative, Aditi, with Vandana, Pushpa, Ashok, Suman, and Kusum ably liaising with our protagonists.

At least 60 per cent of Delhi's population lives in bastis, or informal neighbourhoods. According to the database for the draft Master Plan for Delhi 2041, informal neighbourhoods in the city comprise a range of categories, including JJ (jhuggi-jhopdi) clusters, JJ resettlement colonies, slum-designated areas, unauthorised colonies and regularised unauthorised colonies (National Institute of Urban Affairs, n.d.). Those who populate these localities are predominantly migrants, with Delhi accounting for the country's second largest number of inter-state migrants after Maharashtra.

The immediate visible impact of the pandemic and the first lockdown of March 25, 2020, at a national level was the vast sea of people rushing out of cities across India, on their way back to their villages and hometowns, many of them on foot. The official estimate puts their number at 10 million, although independent analysts believe it could have been twice or thrice that figure (Mander, 2020). A year later, during the second wave, Delhi alone saw a little over 1.3 million leave the city after the second lockdown was announced by Delhi's Chief Minister, Arvind Kejriwal, on April 19, 2021 (Bhardwaj, 2021). In our conversations with residents of the Delhi bastis, what came through clearly was the conundrum they were faced with when the lockdowns were announced. "What played in our minds, most of all, was the question of whether we should return to our village or stay back, even if there was no food at home," recalled Tukli Kol, a widow and mother of two children, Rajesh, 14, and Seema, 12. The family lives in Jagdamba Camp in Sheikh Sarai, South Delhi.

Weighing the options was in itself a tortuous process. As Tukli put it, "When the first lockdown was announced in March 2020, we decided we will try and manage by remaining here. We thought that this, after all, was only a temporary situation and that the lockdown would soon be lifted and life would return to normal." There was also free food being distributed by a local Member of the Legislative Assembly (MLA) and although the family had to stand for long hours in interminable queues to access a plate, there was at least some support. But as the lockdown dragged on and accessing jobs began to appear impossible, "a boundless fear gripped me", Tukli Kol said. "Slowly we noticed people starting to pack up and leave. That filled us with even more anxiety. I then asked myself, 'What will become of me and my children should everyone in our basti leave?'" Her voice trembled as she recaptured that moment. Ultimately, when people from her village in Bengal started making preparations to go back, she knew she had to make up her mind. So she packed up her things and joined, along with her two children, a large group of returning migrants.

Standing in queues for interminable lengths of time became routine for most. This is a group of unemployed workers waiting in line for a plate of food being distributed by a local charity.

When his painting jobs in Delhi vanished, Dharma Singh, a divorced painter in his late 40s from Kanpur, living in the homeless shelter (one of four) in the Yamuna Pushta area, knew he had to leave the city. The only reason that had brought him here was the work the city provides for casual labourers like him. Singh recalled, "No one knew about the lockdown. Once it was announced, we faced problem after problem. I was getting steady jobs as a painter, earning at a rate of Rs 400 per day. These dried up, *ek dum* (suddenly). The *malik* (employer) gave us what we were owed—Rs 4,000 to the two of us working for him—and told us to pack up and leave. So my workmate and I split the amount. I then tried looking for work. No job was too small, no wage too little, but there was literally nothing to be found. The city was dead. So I decided it would be better to go back to Kanpur, where I have a brother at least."

After shelling out Rs 550 from his savings, Singh was lucky to be able to get a seat on a bus headed home. Over the following six months, he survived there, eating as little as he could. It was only in October 2020 that he could return, with the hope that the wedding and festival seasons would produce some painting jobs again. Dharma Singh's journey to Kanpur took around eight hours; he did not find it too difficult to make it back, despite the intense heat and the crowded bus.

For Tukli Kol, it was a different story. The three-day journey to her village proved hellish. She related her experiences with a deadpan expression, but the trauma seeped through her words, "I paid Rs 4,000 for a seat in the bus. They did not charge extra for the children, but the three of us had to squeeze into one seat. The bus people had packed 200 people into a vehicle that was meant to carry 70 at the most. Within a few hours, the overcrowding began to make me sick. There was no air to breathe; everyone was vomiting all over each other. This was at the height of summer too. There was no air-conditioning and it was so hot during the day that the inside of the bus was like a *bhatti* (oven). I almost passed out. I was in such a state that I could hear my children tell people that they thought their mother had died. We could not eat anything during the entirety of those three days even if we wanted to, because of the nausea. To make matters worse, every now and then, the bus would be stopped by the police, who demanded money from the driver to allow him to proceed. This filled every passenger with panic."

The tribulations of that nightmare may perhaps have been worthwhile, if conditions back home were more congenial. But that was not the case, said Tukli Kol. "We realised immediately that people there were also under terrible strain. *Bura hal tha* (it was a terrible situation). Nobody had any money, everyone was bitter and hard up. If a relative gave you a meal, they would do so with gritted teeth and a curse under their breath."

Tukli eked out an existence in her small dwelling unit in the village, with its burning tin roof, as best as she could. In

January 2021, she decided to return to Delhi with her young daughter—but after making the difficult decision to leave her older child behind. "I did this because I knew regaining a foothold in Delhi would be extremely tough, and this way there would be one less mouth to feed," she explained. Once she was back in Delhi, Tukli Kol was constantly worried about her son back in the village, "I had told him, these are difficult times, so whatever we have, we will have to share and survive. But I have not been able to send him money and I worry about how he is managing."

The pandemic forced many in the basti to make such pragmatic but heart-wrenching decisions. Putul of the Lal Gumbad basti—which lies cheek by jowl with the upscale locality of Sadhana Enclave in South Delhi—had also sent her older son back to the village to live with her husband's family. She believed that he would be able to study better there for the Class 12 board examinations, while her younger son, Sandeep, remained with her.

Saleka Begum, Tukli's close friend and a widow like her living two doors away in Jagdamba Camp in Sheikh Sarai, also made similar choices driven by economic compulsions. She, too, left for her village. She returned to Delhi with her younger daughter Pinky in early 2021, leaving her elder daughter, Nasreen, then studying in Class 11, back in the village. As in the case of Tukli Kol, the child left behind needed support. Every two months, Rs 3,000 had to be sent for Nasreen's education, with occasional unexpected additional expenditures, such as when the school insisted that girls in the higher classes wear saris. In Delhi, the mother and younger daughter basically managed on a single proper meal, cooking only once a day.

When Naresh, a resident of Jagdamba Camp, lost his job as a *safai karamchari* (sanitation worker) in a private hospital in Sheikh Sarai after the first lockdown, going back to the village seemed like the sensible thing to do, given the lack of a regular income. What dissuaded him was the lack of public transport at that point; he also kept hearing news about the police beating up people on the road. But by the second lockdown in April 2021, the situation in Delhi had become impossible and his family was forced to head back to the village. However, this decision did not help ease the family's financial crisis as they had hoped it would; in fact, the decision only exacerbated it. Naresh ruefully remarked, "What we did not bargain for was the expense involved. Journeys like that don't come cheap. That trip cost the family Rs 50,000 and drove us even deeper into debt."

The link between the village and the city, once strong, invariably becomes attenuated as time goes by, in spite of regular phone calls and the occasional visit. Everybody initially came to Delhi in search of a better life, and for a chance to climb out of the poverty trap for the sake of their children. Sushila of Lal Gumbad explained, "My husband, Rajesh, and I are from Rae Barelli, Uttar Pradesh. He came to Delhi in 2001, and when I married him in 2008, I came over too. He had four brothers. Their family had two and half *bighas* of land (about one and half acres). In effect this amounted to nothing. So you could say he was forced to come to Delhi in search of a livelihood."

When she first came to this basti, where they have always lived, Sushila found everything extremely dirty and difficult. Even the water—when it came, that is—seemed muddy. Slowly she got used to the pace of the city and the clockwork regimen it imposed upon people. She said, "I would get up at 5:00 a.m. and go to the community toilet, where one had to wait in a queue. Earlier, women had to pay Re 1 every time they went, and the men Rs 2. Now this user fee has been lifted, so that is a relief—although toilets used to be cleaner then. After this, I would make *nashta* (breakfast) for my husband, who works in a paper mill in Okhla. I would also make a few extra rotis for his lunch—around 12 rotis in all. He would leave home around 8:15 a.m. and return around 6:00 p.m., unless he had overtime duty—then, he would return around 10:00 p.m. Meanwhile, I would work in rich people's homes. Together, we could earn Rs 20,000 or so; we could even afford to send Rs 2,000 to my mother-in-law in the village every month until she passed away. Now, everything has become *ulta pulta* (upside down). We really have to scramble to get even half of what we once earned. We have lost every little gain we made by coming to Delhi. We are back in penury with a debt of Rs 30,000 and a monthly rent of Rs 3,500 to pay."

Some basti residents, living in their cramped tenements, regard the lives they left behind in the village through an idyllic lens. Nujita Bano looked around her tiny room in Jagdamba Camp and exclaimed, "Everything is so confined here. This room we have is so tiny and it doesn't even have a window. At least back home in the village, even though we were poor, we had open fields and open skies around us."

Ayaan, Rehan and Parveen, Nujita Bano's three little ones in her tiny one-room tenement. Many months of rent were always outstanding for the family during the pandemic because her husband had no job.

It is in times of crisis at either end that old ties get renewed. As Chanchal, a resident of Lal Gumbad, explained, "Our village is in Jaunpur district of UP; we came to Delhi some 16 years ago. Although we have had our own difficulties here, we have always been responsive to the difficulties of relatives back home. My husband's mud house in the village got badly damaged during floods. This meant that my mother-in-law and sister-in-law had to move into a relative's house, where they were given a roof in exchange for their domestic labour. We feel terrible about this, because my sister-in-law, who was then in Class 10, had to give up schooling. Now we want to help with her marriage, but that would mean a sum of at least two lakhs. How do we get such money? Each poor family has its own struggles to cope with."

As Tukli Kol noted, with the pandemic, people back in the village were not exactly eager to welcome back long-lost relatives. Dharma Singh doesn't mince words: "This *mahamari* (pandemic) is such a period that there is just no sharing of others' problems. Each person is caught up in their own world of suffering. It is a situation where even brothers cannot look after their brothers. It is each one for himself."

The city had also grown crueller; its ways were created to exclude rather than include. New rules now laid down that one would have to first furnish proof of having been in Delhi for at least a year before she or he can apply for any welfare provision. This left people making endless rounds of government offices to get the required documents and being constantly told to come back the next day. They were asked to present their *bijli ka bill* (electricity bill) but could not do so because their landlords wouldn't give it to them for fear that their tenants would claim ownership of the property. Those in rented accommodations—which made up the great majority of the Delhi bastis—were the most vulnerable, and lived in dread of losing the very roof over their heads.

These conversations revealed the big slide back into poverty of the majority of families during the pandemic. Any hope of a better life, wholesome food, regular education for the children—which appeared to have reached a point of realisation—had now all but faded. Even the sanctuary of the old home in the village appeared uncertain.

Today, most basti residents have put on mortgage anything valuable they had, like the gold chain that a Jagdamba Camp resident gave as surety for a loan of Rs 15,000 and which she has not been able to redeem. Almost everybody we spoke to had a similar story to relate, while the mounting debt cast a long shadow on their peace of mind and their future.

Chapter 2

When the Door Slams on You…The Crisis of Finding Work

Women in the bastis refer to their employer colloquially as the *kothi wali*, or the *memsahib* who lives in a proper home, the floors of which the women sweep and scrub every day to earn a living. There is significant distance between the *kothi wali* and the *basti wali*, reflected in spatial terms: the genteel leafy neighbourhood with parks and broad roads, where the *kothi wali* lives, presents a study in contrast to the living environs of the *basti wali*, with its unplastered brick-walled dwellings, tightly packed together and crisscrossed by narrow pathways, drains gurgling with murky water. The difference is also emphasised by their respective locations in the caste-class hierarchy.

The pandemic—given that everybody was equally susceptible to its dread impacts—affected both sides of this divide, but its effects were by no means equal. While the lives and livelihood of the *basti wali* were devastated beyond measure, the *kothi wali*—protected by a carapace of wealth, connections, and facilities—could cope far better with the crisis. The *kothi wali-basti wali* relationship has always been marked by opportunism, with the first category drawing on the cheap labour of the second as an answer to the burden of performing the endless household chores that fall upon her by virtue of being a wife, a mother, a woman. Yet, as panic over the virus, along with ill-informed rumours and speculation,

Women in the bastis refer to their employer colloquially as the *kothi wali*. The *kothi wali* and the *basti wali* inhabit two different worlds, and the distance between them only grew during the pandemic.

gripped the city by the third week of March 2020, and the population was advised to observe "social distancing" and WFH—the trendy acronym for "work from home"—the *basti wali*, who could not work from home, metamorphosed into a source of contagion for the *kothi wali*.

Putul, of Lal Gumbad basti, recalled, "The day after the lockdown, when I reported for duty, my *memsahib* told me that she cannot keep me anymore because I stayed in a basti and I could spread the virus. She did not want me to touch her family's dishes or cook their food, or even be physically present while the disease was around. She was willing, though, to hire me as a full-time maid, but then I would have to stay with her family, and would not be allowed to go back to my own home for a long while. Even though I was desperate for a regular income, I could not do that. Who would look after my family? Who would run my home?"

Without realising the importance of her words, Putul was articulating the double burden of the domestic worker. The household work she performs for her employer are also chores that she has to tackle in her own home. According to data from Dalberg Research, while Indian women performed 6.5 hours of unpaid work before the pandemic—three times more than men— there was a 47 per cent increase in such labour during the pandemic (Dalberg Advisors, 2021).

The household work on offer for the women of the Delhi bastis is broadly of two kinds: tasks like cleaning dishes, washing clothes, dusting, sweeping and mopping floors, are paid by the hour, and exhausting though they may be, it is possible for someone to work in several homes on a single day. The other system is what was being offered to Putul: full-time occupation that could stretch for 12 hours but implicit in the arrangement is the understanding that the worker is at the beck and call of her employers at all times while she resides in their home.

A family enjoying a rare moment of leisure after the morning chores have been completed.

It is important to note here, that both these versions of domestic work are unregulated and working conditions are dictated largely by the employers, who are secure not just in their financial status, but in the knowledge that there is a large pool of working class women in search of work available to them. It is the informal nature of the work conducted within the private sphere that adds to the oppression of the "madam-maid" relationship. The pandemic brought out the full spectrum of the inequalities that it was marked by.

Almost every woman in the bastis, who worked as household help, had remarkably similar experiences to relate. After the first lockdown was announced, many were not even allowed to enter the houses where they had once worked, and were turned away by guards who peremptorily informed them to come back after the *mahamari* was over. One woman recalled, "I had tied my dupatta over my mouth and stood some distance away, but I was just shooed away as if I were the disease." Those who were able to get past the guards had to interact with their employers standing behind closed doors, or speaking through glass-paned windows. In such a situation, it was impossible to explain one's predicament clearly, and it was always the *memsahib* who had the last word. Several euphemisms were employed by them. Older workers were told that given their advancing years, perhaps it would be best that they now take some rest. Women with young children were advised to devote their time to keeping their families safe by staying at home. Such advice reflected how little these women of privilege understood about the realities of the lives of those who worked for them, and for whom staying idle was not a choice.

Sushila put it this way, "I used to work in two or three houses. After the first lockdown, most of the *kothi walis* paid us our dues promptly and told us that they would call us when they wanted us back. Only one among the three in whose homes I had worked offered to pay me half my wages until I resumed. The others didn't seem to even consider how we would be able to feed our families without a regular salary although we had done so much for their families all these many years." Only a single act of kindness was reported in all our conversations. Saleka Begum of Jagdamba Camp informed us that one of her employers had given her 25 kilos of rice to help her tide over the emergency situation.

All through the months of unemployment and hunger, no one reported receiving a call from their employers to inquire about how they were doing. On the contrary, when they tried to call their employers to find out when they could resume work, their calls remained unanswered or were blocked. After the first lockdown eased somewhat and it seemed possible to access work once again, attempts to re-establish contact began in earnest. The intervening months had seen many changes. Since they didn't have any money for public conveyance and the like, many domestic workers from the bastis, who would have earlier taken a bus trip or shared an autorickshaw, now had no option but to walk long distances to their places of employment.

There was also the possibility of their employers having shifted out in the intervening period. "When I went back, I found that the family that I had worked for had relocated somewhere else, and I had to search all over again for another job," remembered Soni of Jagdamba Camp. The number of jobs available had come down drastically. In many cases, salaries were scaled down by the employers, who pleaded their own straitened circumstances because of loss of income and employment during the pandemic. There were also arguments over the old dues to be collected. One woman remarked, "They have so much more money than us but they will constantly bargain to get the better of you. *Arrey*, we are poor women, even if by mistake you give us an extra rupee, will it really hurt you?"

The lack of equality between employer and employee manifested itself in subtle but important ways, even after resumption of work. On the one hand, while the employee was surveilled and constantly asked if the situation at home was COVID-19-free, it wasn't reciprocal. On the other, only 5 per cent of respondents of a phone survey of 75 domestic workers in New Delhi and Gurugram, conducted in December 2020 by researchers Prashansa Srivastava and Prachi Shukla, had information about outbreaks of the infection at their places of work, with many pointing out that employers did not seem to feel the obligation to inform their domestic workers if any of their family members was infected or was showing symptoms of the virus (Srivastava and Shukla, 2021).

The intervening period of skimping on meals had taken a toll on the health of many. Saleka Begum, who had a pre-existing condition of severe anaemia, now found the long trek to her employer's house a huge challenge. "Once work resumed, I would leave home early and walk slowly to the place, stopping every now and then. Even if one was exhausted, there was no question of skipping work. I was so worried I would lose my job after all those days of unemployment that I made it a point to carry on no matter how bad I felt," she recalled. Employment surveys all point to how it was women who lost out the most in terms of employment during the pandemic (N. Neetha, 2021). More specific data reveals that within this category it was domestic workers who were the slowest to regain employment (Srivastava and Shukla, 2021).

There were other adjustments to be made as well. In Yashoda's home, for instance, the pandemic period had seen the addition of a new member of the family—little Shaghun was born in June 2020. "Now, once I went back to work after the first lockdown, I had to think about how the baby was to be cared for while I was away. My oldest, Sangeeta, who turned 11, has now learnt to take care of the infant," explained Yashoda. When asked about how this might affect Sangeeta's schooling, Yashoda explained that since school had not started for her and since the family did not have a smartphone, there was no possibility of online classes for her in any case. Arrangements of this kind reveal how the exploitative aspect of the madam-maid relationship could extend to the latter's entire family.

The job market is deeply marked by caste-stratifications, even in a cosmopolitan metropolis like Delhi. Meeting Naresh—who is in his 50s and has a room in Jagdamba Camp—provided an insight into how caste identities deeply marked the nature of the kind of jobs that were available. He was one of those "corona warriors" much feted during the early days of the pandemic for doing the hard and dangerous work of sanitising hospital premises and their environs. "I worked for a private hospital to clean up and disinfect those areas where the sick had gathered, like ambulances, waiting areas, lift lobbies. Once the crowds began to grow, it was a very tough time for people like us. I found myself exhausted all the time. I won't lie—I really wanted to quit the job and look for something better, but it brought in valuable money."

Naresh was proud of his abilities. Although he was consigned to the periphery of the hospital's activities, much was happening in the peripheral area at that point as severely ill people waited to be admitted. He learnt to be of assistance during crucial junctures such as assisting in the administration of oxygen to breathless patients. His dream was to make it further into the core services of the hospital as a medical attendant who is required to take blood samples, assist nursing staff, and so on. That, however, was not to be.

"One day my supervisor dismissed me without giving me a reason. I think this is because he wanted his own person in. This led to a severe crisis at home because even my wife, who was working as a house help, had no employment. Our expenses were mounting, as was our debt: the rent itself was Rs 2,500, plus electricity charges of another Rs 500. There were absolutely no jobs available at that time—my sandals wore out as I went from place to place asking for some source of livelihood." As Naresh related this, tears gathered in his eyes, the trauma of those days writ large on his face. After many days of hunting, he finally managed a job as a "house help". In effect, he had become a domestic worker for a well-off family in an

Naresh, a hospital *karamchari* (worker), lost his job during the pandemic. After failing to procure work, he finally got a position as "house help".

upmarket neighbourhood. But once again, his tasks were confined to the periphery of the house, with all interactions with the family strictly limited and controlled. The money he makes is not what he used to earn in the hospital but at least it pays for the rent.

What comes through in the conversations with domestic workers is how society, the labour markets and state policies, together create conditions for their dehumanisation. In August 2021, we caught up with Gulab Chand, *istriwala* (ironing man), who had pitched his makeshift stall near the Lal Gumbad basti once again. After several months of being idle, he finally has some work as a small bundle of clothes near his feet, waiting to be ironed, indicated. He used a colloquial idiom to explain his experience of joblessness during the lockdowns, "People were sitting at home during the lockdown and didn't need ironed clothes, so who would want

Gulab Chand, who earns a living ironing clothes, could set up his makeshift shed only after the pandemic. He remarked, "We felt like wheat being ground in a *chakki* (mill)".

my services? Truly the pandemic ground us down like wheat in the *chakki* (mill)."

Through it all, what was also evident and needs to be emphasised was the quality of resilience and courage displayed by those "ground down like wheat" in the face of what was an unprecedented and devastating personal crisis.

Chapter 3
The Parallel Pandemic of Hunger

The first sight a visitor to any basti during the pandemic is greeted by is that of children of all ages—who should normally have been at school—running around, laughing, screaming, quarrelling, playing. Their voices fill the air and speak of hope, even amidst the spread of a virus that has utterly altered their lives in ways which they seem barely conscious of.

Shut classrooms meant a lot more play time for the basti children, and kite flying was a favourite pastime.

Mothers speak of how their children adjusted to a new reality: ever-present hunger. The *mahamari* of malnutrition ran parallel to that caused by the COVID-19 virus. The period between March 2020 and July 2021 saw two waves of COVID-19 and two lockdowns resulting in a calamitous loss of livelihood. With purses quickly emptying out amidst rising prices and inadequate welfare measures, chronic hunger was an inevitable consequence.

The majority of families living in Delhi's bastis belong to the lower castes and have already suffered generations of malnutrition and undernutrition. In a 2020 paper titled, "Which Indian Children are Short and Why? Social Identity, Childhood Malnutrition and Cognitive Outcomes", Ashwini Deshpande and Rajesh Ramchandran established the shorter height-for-age of children from the lower-ranked and stigmatised castes based on data of 213,000 children (Deshpande and Ramachandran, 2020). The pandemic has only added another dimension of deprivation to this stark reality.

Yashoda of Lal Gumbad basti summed up the situation baldly, "My children have given up the habit of eating." Strange as this observation may sound, it is by no means a rare one. Another woman we engaged in casual conversation with in Jagdamba Camp, who was trying to get her frisky 10-year-old son to have a bath on a sweltering August morning, complained in a tone of irritation mixed with maternal indulgence, "He is always running here and there. He doesn't even come for food. The moment he eats, he falls ill." Other women spoke of how terrible they felt when their children asked for an extra something, a small treat now and then. It hurt them to say no, but they had no choice in the matter.

These are children who have experienced a double deprivation. The 20 months of schooling that they lost have combined with 20 months of nutritional loss. In fact, the very material impact of classrooms having turned virtual during the period of the pandemic had meant the disappearance of the crucial midday meal in the lives of millions of children across the country. Mothers in the

A mother after she had just got her son to have a bath in the communal toilet. The child spent all his time playing, hardly coming home to eat the food his mother made because it was so unappetising.

Delhi bastis pointed to the irony of the situation: at a time when they were struggling to feed their children—when that one meal provided free of charge by the State assumed even greater value in their lives than in normal times—was precisely when it became unavailable.

In December 2020, the Delhi government promised to provide dry rations for six months in lieu of the midday meal that school children had been deprived of during the lockdown. Yet, from our conversations, it was clear that not many benefitted from this step. Lack of documentation proved to be a huge obstacle in this instance too. According to one mother, two of her three children received some money in their account and a one-time ration kit. Her third child, in Class 5, received nothing at all because he was born in the village and the family did not have a birth certificate for him, because of which they could not get an Aadhaar card made in his name. The parents spent a lot of money, trying very hard to procure a birth certificate for him, but to little avail.

Anita, who lives in the Lal Gumbad basti, has three children: Nithin, 13, Ayush, 11, and Arav, 4. Because Ayush was registered in the local government school, the family received a one-time school ration packet consisting of four kilos each of *chana dal* (split peas), wheat, and rice, along with one kilo of *dalda* (hydrogenated fat). Anita was thankful for this assistance but had serious problems with the *dalda*: "It's of no use. If you make *parathas* out of them, a white layer forms on top, and the children fall ill after eating them."

In such a period of stress, every grain mattered, every paisa had value. Earlier, things were far easier. Yashoda explained, "Before the *mahamari*, both my husband and I worked—he ran a food handcart and I did *jaadhu-pocha* in a few homes—and together, we earned around Rs 16,000. This allowed us to have three full meals a day: *dal-chawal, sabzi-roti*. Occasionally—once a week or so—we used to have *parathas*, eggs, chicken. Now, we have had to cut out one meal, and eat either plain rice or plain *rotis*, with some *alu chokka* (seasoned potato) occasionally."

The daily diet for everybody had become strongly correlated to family income. As money became scarcer, so too did the quality and quantity of the food they ate. The first meal of the day—breakfast or *nashta*—which nutritionists consider vital for health, had been completely dispensed with: "*Hum naashta nahin karte* (we don't eat breakfast)," said Yashoda emphatically. She has three children: Sangeeta, 11, Ayush, 6, and Shaghun, 1. Since Yashoda cannot feed the baby herself given her own poor diet, the family invests, with great difficulty, in a half a litre packet of double toned milk from the nearby Mother Dairy booth. This is stretched out for three to four days. Milk is for the baby only. Yashoda doesn't remember the last time she or anyone else in the family had milk with their tea. Her husband too, whom she referred to as a "good man", came under severe pressure to earn something; he began to suffer from health problems, including severe headaches. A hospital test revealed that he had very low blood pressure. Yashoda was convinced that his condition was triggered by the fact that he had to donate blood while not eating properly, in order to get hospital admission.

Yashoda with her three children, Sangeeta, Ayush and Shagun, in her one-room home. Shagun was born during the first wave, and the family had no money to take care of the pregnant mother.

Nujita Bano, who came from Bihar and stayed in Jagdamba Camp, reeled out a list of items she did not have: "Right now, in my house, there is no oil, no wheat, no rice, no tea powder. We live from day to day on whatever little my husband gives me and the shopkeepers

Nujita with little Parveen, who had hurt herself grievously during the pandemic. Her mother was in a panic because the public hospital had become a COVID centre. Fortunately, she found a doctor to stitch up her child's bleeding forehead.

loan me." With three small children, all below 5 years, she could not work, and her husband had been unable to earn what he once did by working as a shop assistant.

Most of the families we came across lacked the all-important ration card that would have allowed them to buy foodgrain at cheaper rates, and therefore, make them less dependent on the occasional handouts that the Delhi government announced from time to time. Many had applied for their ration cards years earlier, but every time they visited the ration office, they were told their application was "pending". In fact, an RTI filed by the Delhi Rozi Roti Adhikar Abhiyan (DRRAA) and Satark Nagrik Sangathan (SNS) in December 2020 revealed that pending ration card applications in Delhi numbered around 1.73 lakh (information gained from a discussion with SNS activists).

Meanwhile, prices of commodities registered a significant rise. "Forget vegetables, they are a luxury, who can afford them at Rs 20 a quarter kilo, but even something as basic as cooking oil has doubled in price. *Sarson ka tel* (mustard oil), which used to cost Rs 80 once, is now Rs 170, and just one egg costs Rs 8. How do we manage? We eat less and less, and mostly only plain rice or *chapati*, that's how," exclaimed Sushila of Lal Gumbad.

The struggle was to somehow keep hunger pangs at bay. Families came up with their own solutions to this dilemma. One mother revealed that she fed her two children a packet of watery Maggi by way of a midday meal. Then, there was a recipe "to stay healthy even when one is hungry," that was proffered by Shyam Sunder Prasad, a 72-year-old who had taken refuge in a shelter for the homeless at Yamuna Pushta: "Sometimes, if people give me some extra money by way of alms, I put loose *chana* (split peas) into a plastic bottle of water. If you eat a handful of soaked raw *chana* first thing in the morning, you feel like you have eaten a full meal. It goes into the stomach and expands. *Moong dal* (unhusked lentil) is also good for this." There was a sharp poignancy in his words—a meal existed almost as an illusion.

Sushila's two sons share a small meal of Maggi noodles to keep the hunger pangs at bay, a common scenario in many homes during this period.

Research has indicated that one of the striking aspects of the meals of the poor during the pandemic has been their lack of "dietary diversity" (Verderosa, 2021). According to a study conducted by the Tata-Cornell Institute for Agriculture and Nutrition during the pandemic period in rural Uttar Pradesh, Bihar and Odisha, "nearly 90 [per cent] of survey respondents reported having less food, while 95 [per cent] said they consumed fewer types of food and less nutritious items" (Verderosa, 2021).

Chanchal Devi of Lal Gumbad basti was open about the pain it caused her to deprive her children of the nutrition they needed. "For months, we haven't been able to give tea with milk to our children although they cannot stomach black tea. Earlier, we would be able to give them milk with Bournvita. Now they eat *rotis* or rice without *sabzi*. My son particularly keeps complaining and says, 'I don't want to eat this or that.' I have to scream at him to get him to eat whatever there is on his plate."

She realised very clearly that this was impacting her children's health; they had lost weight before her eyes, "Once in a way, I try to get something extra—the other day a vendor came to our locality to sell overripe mangoes at Rs 20 a kilo and I bought a few just to give them something new. We have a small fridge, but there is nothing in it today!"

A stroke of luck visited her in July 2021 when, after *Bloomberg* magazine featured her family, representatives of a political party came to her door, bearing two large bags of wheat flour and rice. "For me, this was like a gift from God. It kept my family fed for a few weeks." In such distressing times, it was only through the generosity of ambitious politicians or conscientious citizens who came forward with free food, that hunger was stemmed for many within these neighbourhoods.

Musarrat Ara, 38, a single mother of two living in a Govindpuri basti, laid bare the deep anxieties that beset her during this period. Deserted by her husband, she has a 17-year-old daughter, Neelu, who suffers from cerebral palsy. Her only source of support is her 19-year-old son, Haider, who had never attended school properly and had started earning for the family as a young boy. Before the pandemic, he worked in a tailoring unit earning Rs 7,000 a month.

"When he lost his job after the first lockdown, my first thought was: how was the family to be fed?" recalled Musarrat. "All three of us would go to a local school where they were distributing free food, and stand for hours in a line to feed ourselves. Every night, I was sleepless, fearful of what the next day would bring, because although we have been living in Delhi for over 25 years, we had no papers to prove it." It was only in late May 2020, when the Delhi High Court instructed the Delhi government to deliver rations to those without ration cards, that Musarrat was able to procure e-coupons with the help of strangers; she came home with five kilos of foodgrain that allowed her to start cooking again.

Keeping the kitchen fire burning meant a great deal of work when one had to manage with so little. Rationed wheat, even when

It took a lot of effort to clean the wheat procured from the public distribution centre. The grain has to be washed and dried, before being milled.

it could be procured, was generally of very poor quality. Hours had to be spent on washing and drying the foodgrain, before it could be milled for the family's consumption.

There were also constant sacrifices to be made. The first to be sold were household effects that had any value at all. Yashoda's husband, for instance, was forced to sell an item that was the foundation of his earnings: his handcart. Soni, of Jagdamba Camp, a mother of five children, recalled the wrench she felt while parting with a gold necklace she got at the time of her marriage—it was used as surety for a loan of Rs 15,000. Since the family did not have the money to pay back that amount, she had now reconciled herself to the prospect of losing forever that piece of jewellery which once held great sentimental value. She was only one of the many who had registered such losses: the country's largest gold loan provider, Manappuram Finance, auctioned the gold it received from bad loans worth $54 million in the three months of March to May 2021 (Bose, 2021).

Mounting debt was an ever-present reality for the majority of families living in Delhi bastis. This was borne out by macroeconomic data from the Reserve Bank of India (RBI) which indicated that, as of March 2021, overall household debt stood at Rs 43.5 trillion in India. Another strategy to cope with impoverished circumstances was to move into cheaper and smaller accommodation. One case of a woman, who did not want to be named, was fairly typical, "We were in a debt of Rs 70,000 at one stage and were not able to pay the rent. Our *makaan malik* (landlord) told us to pack up. We found another place in the same locality that was smaller and slightly cheaper but we still had to pay Rs 3,000 for one room, plus electricity charges." Paying the rent on time even after that move continues to be a challenge for her. "We are now late with our rent money all over again," she remarked.

Among other strategies that families adopted in the face of the dark future facing them was to marry away their female children prematurely. The year 2020, according to the National Crime Records Bureau (NCRB) data, witnessed child marriages rise by 50 per cent in comparison to 2019 (News18, 2021). In addition, children from poorer families in situations such as the pandemic were always under the threat of being sucked into the labour market. Going by the stories we heard, sometimes, after realising the huge stress on their parents in terms of procuring food and paying for the rent, the children had themselves opted for small jobs to bring in extra income.

But what may initially have been regarded as a temporary measure became permanent over time: the children may never go back to the classroom. The ILO-UNICEF report, "COVID-19 and child labour: A time of crisis, a time to act" (ILO-UNICEF, 2020), noted that while the negative consequences of school disruption during the pandemic may be limited for those with some means, very poor families may come to regard the supplementary income their children are bringing in as essential to their survival and discontinue their schooling altogether (ibid.). This pandemic of hunger, going by our conversations in the bastis, is then not just about deprivation of food. Hunger had cascading economic and social consequences for the poorest and most marginalised.

Chapter 4
Suffering Domestic Violence in a Well of Silence

Let us call her "Sarika". This is not her real name but the experiences she relates are not fiction. Unfortunately, they are not uncommon either. There are many Sarikas in the bastis of Delhi, bearing the burden of a ubiquitous trauma and often tell-tale physical bruises, even as they go about their daily chores like everyone else. The Delhi-based women's resource group, Jagori, reported that within a couple of months of the March 2020 lockdown, women were affirming an increase in domestic violence, including violence inflicted by marital and natal families. One of the significant reasons cited was emotional and financial stress caused by physical confinement due to the lockdown (Jagori, 2020).

Sarika comes from a family of migrants, with her father having opted to leave his village in Rajasthan to find work in Delhi some 40 years earlier. She herself was born in this city some five years after that arrival. In fact, she is one of the few women we met who possessed a ration card. After she got married around 14 years ago, she moved into the room owned by her husband in the basti and today the couple has three children, the eldest of whom suffers from a serious disability.

Sarika began with these words: "When I married him, he was a decent man. It was after my eldest was born 13 years ago that he first started taking to drink. Initially, he drank in moderation and things were okay between us. But over the years, he became increasingly addicted." Alcohol use disorder is defined as a condition characterised by a recurring desire on the part of the individual to imbibe liquor despite knowing that it has severely harmful consequences (Cleveland Clinic, n.d.).

"Once he became a *bewda* (drunkard), he just could not retain a job. Today he is reduced to working as a *mazdoor* (casual labourer) but the family gets very little from his earnings. No matter what he makes, whether it is Rs 400 a day or double that amount, he just drinks it all away. He can drink away any amount. In the morning, he may seem fine, leave the house saying he is going for work, but he will return around 10:00 p.m. every night totally drunk," Sarika's tone was divorced from all emotion. Her husband's drinking set the pattern of Sarika's life. The responsibility of feeding a growing family fell almost entirely on her shoulders. Her two older sisters, who also happened to have homes in the same neighbourhood, were her only source of support.

These difficult conditions turned insufferable once the first lockdown was implemented in March 2020. "Suddenly all my sources of income as a household help dried up—my employers did not want an outsider in their homes during the *mahamari*, and told me to rejoin only after it was over. For the next six months, I could not earn a single paisa. My husband, who would earlier at least leave the house in search of work, was now constantly around and constantly drinking. I was in total depression," recalled Sarika. Studies have shown how a situation of substance abuse and domestic violence, combined with home isolation, increases the threat of a multitude of psychiatric diseases (Mental Health in the Times of COVID-19 Pandemic, 2020). In the bastis of Delhi, these conditions generally remain below the surface, but manifest themselves in vicious brawls, including those between spouses.

With time on his hands, Sarika's husband made all kinds of unrealistic demands on her: "He would insist I cook something 'nice' for him and would scream at me when I failed to do so. I would tell him that first, he has to give me some money to run the house, otherwise it is impossible for me to provide appetising food for him. I would immediately get beaten for what he considered to be my insolence." Every time the situation reached a breaking point, Sarika would escape, along with her children, to her sisters' homes, "If my sisters had not been there, I don't know what I would have done. They are so good to me, always helping out. But I know, eventually, this is a situation that I have to cope with alone. No outsider can do anything about it."

Any money that she managed to get by borrowing from her sisters, he would grab from her and spend on his liquor. It had now become an unending cycle of violence and abuse, with the children huddled in one corner of the room, not knowing what to do. As the "master" of the house, the drunken man would deny his wife her basic freedom of movement. He would do this either by preventing her from going out, guarding the door and beating her if she tried to escape, or by locking her out if she was successful in her attempt to flee. Sometimes, when she was locked out without the children, she would be terrified about their fate, "What if he hurts them badly? What if my eldest, who is disabled, does bathroom and there is no one to clean up after him? Sometimes what I feared the most would come true. He would shout at the children and thrash them but thankfully, so far, he has left my eldest one alone. He—poor boy—is incapable of understanding the situation."

The layout of her home makes the situation even more dangerous. Sarika stays in a room on the second floor of a row of tenements in the basti, which can only be reached by climbing two steep flights of stairs. Sometimes when her husband hit her and she got into a scuffle with him, she feared that she would fall down the stairwell and break her neck.

The stairs in the basti are often steep and without hand railings. The biggest fear Sarika had when she was attacked by her drunken husband was falling down the stairs and breaking her neck.

The houses in the basti are in close proximity with each other, and the neighbours can certainly overhear all the terrifying sounds of these episodic bouts of domestic violence. They generally however, choose not to interfere, leaving the assaulters to have their way.

We asked Sarika whether she ever tried to call the police. Her answer was prompt, "Not just once, several times. I know the Delhi Police number—100. They have even turned up at the door on a couple of occasions. But it did not help." In any case, according to Sarika, the police—perhaps because they have witnessed so many cases of this kind after the lockdown began— treat such *mara mari* (beating) as "normal in any marriage". As she put it, "They would just warn my husband to behave himself, threaten him with imprisonment if he beats me again, and go away. In fact, every time they left, my husband would start beating me even more for bringing *beizzati* (dishonour) upon him."

The interminable drinking bouts have led to the sharp rise of the family's debt, "Since he never has money to buy what he wants, he borrows from anyone who can spare some money. One day he took my gold earring tops—they weighed five grams and must have cost around Rs 14,000 when they were given to me at the time of my marriage—to the *bania* (money lender). He assured me that he will get them back, but that was the last I saw of them."

Since her husband was not earning anything and was constantly looking for money to buy a drink, the habit of borrowing small sums of money from people, even strangers, became very marked during the pandemic. Those who lent him the money would later confront Sarika, demanding repayment, "I would tell them plainly that I have no money to give them but sometimes they would threaten me and the children. Although I put up a brave front, such confrontations make me very nervous and scared. My husband also gets into fights, and I often have to intervene and take him away before he gets badly beaten up."

Was there no one to counsel her husband, we asked. Her reply was unambiguous—there was absolutely no one, "My husband's friends are just like him, and they must also be behaving like him in their own homes, preying on their wives."

While the pandemic may have declined in intensity, the negative impacts of aggregated domestic violence it witnessed will remain with women like Sarika for the rest of their lives. She maintains that there is no escape for her, "I worry about the future of my children constantly. I cannot leave my husband. Where will I go with the kids? At least now they have a roof over their heads. My eldest son won't be able to look after himself for all his life. The one younger than him is very smart, but because we only have a button-*wala* phone, he has not been able to do online classes. The youngest boy is only 4, and it doesn't matter so much that he is not studying. But I have to keep going. I have now started working in homes and begun to earn some money regularly. I would like to take up more jobs but circumstances at home make this impossible."

Domestic violence in the family has also marked the children; Sarika discerned this instinctively. "Once, my second son, who is only 11, picked up a stick to hit his father when he was attacking me. The boy has grown up seeing violence and has learnt to accept it as part of life. He keeps saying that when he becomes big he will teach his father a lesson. I don't like to hear this. It hurts me because I know that he could become violent in the future, beat other people and get into trouble. But what can I do? This, after all, is the effect my husband's drinking has on each of our lives," she remarked.

Sarika's narrative indicated the disturbing isolation of women like her even in situations where their very physical existence was under threat. Psychiatrists maintain that the damage domestic violence unleashes on the assaulted, the assaulter and those closely involved like children, is permanent. It leads to conditions like Post-Traumatic Stress Disorder (PTSD) and suicidal tendencies. Children who have experienced it either actively or passively—for instance, by watching their mothers get beaten—could suffer severe emotional shocks in the immediate aftermath, or even years later (Cunningham and Baker, n.d.).

While there has been significant international and national recognition of the "shadow pandemic" of domestic violence during the COVID-19 crisis, public response to it in India has been underwhelming. The policies the Delhi government chose to implement during this period point to this apathy. While it never failed to present itself as a "caring government", even setting up a 13-member committee to come up with an action plan to handle a possible third wave of COVID-19, such concern seems to shrink significantly when weighed against prospects of earning additional revenue.

Liberalising liquor sales was one of the most conspicuous ways in which the Delhi government addressed the significant hit it suffered financially over two successive lockdowns. This state-enabled expansion of liquor markets was done without wider consultation with the public or any consideration of the possible consequences that such a policy would have at the societal and family levels.

The announcement of the first lockdown on March 25, 2020, brought down the shutters on liquor outlets throughout the country. By May 4 of that year, sales were resumed in Delhi with some curtailment of the time allowed for vends to stay open. The next day, an additional "Corona fee" on alcohol sales was imposed which amounted to 70 per cent of the maximum retail price of the product (Special Correspondent, 2020). By May 30, the Delhi government was successful in generating Rs 234.54 crore from liquor sales, with an additional mop-up of Rs 160 crore from the Corona levy. For the state government, liquor sales became central to its financial calculations, an approach made apparent in its budget for the year 2020–21, where 14 per cent of tax revenue—or Rs 6,300 crore—was projected to come from this source (Mondal, 2020). In the days that followed, every attempt was made by the Delhi government to expand alcohol sales and lower the threshold of difficulty in its procurement for the ordinary consumer. From August 8, 2020, it allowed liquor shops to function from 10:00 a.m. to 10:00 p.m., which was the pre-pandemic duration. Ten months later, it even allowed the home delivery of alcohol.

Women in the bastis are no trained economists. They may not make the connection between a government policy to liberalise liquor sales and the flailing fist back home. But they realise something that the government does not: the easy availability of alcohol at a time when families were at their most vulnerable has damaged their lives in ways they cannot even put into words.

Chapter 5

Locked Classrooms Leave
Young Lives in Limbo

Are online classes better than those conducted in a classroom? A stray question put to a group of children in a Delhi basti—all of them between the ages of 9 and 11—indicates how intuitively the children grasped the value of school, which they have not been attending since March 2020. Schools in Delhi finally opened in offline mode in February 2022, but it will take a long while to evaluate the losses inflicted by the pandemic on their schooling.

The poignant and impromptu conversation conducted on the roof of a small dwelling overlooking the late thirteenth-century Lal Gumbad in August 2021, remains etched in the memory because it reveals the many ways in which the pandemic had left young lives in a limbo.

Priya, 11, her eyes all aglow, set off the discussion by remarking about why she just loved going to school, "In school I have my best friend and we talk all the time." Her sister, Pallavi, all of 9, interrupted her with a tentative observation that online may be better because "ma'am cannot scold us". Her suggestion was roundly dismissed by 10-year-old Sandeep, a neighbour, "Ma'am also scolds us online and tells us that she will stop teaching us if we don't pay attention. So it's not true that we get scolded less during online classes."

Priya, 11, and Pallavi, 9, both missed school during the lockdown. The 11-year-old says, "We miss our friends terribly and ma'am gives us a lot of homework during online classes."

Meanwhile, Priya came up with a more substantial argument as to why nothing can better the actual classroom, "Online we have to sit and listen, and ma'am gives us a lot of homework to do. In school too, we are given homework, but then we can ask ma'am if we are not able to do it properly. In school, ma'am writes on the blackboard and we can read slowly, and understand what she tells us clearly. It's not the same online, because even if you have a doubt, you cannot clear it properly."

Pallavi, now on the side that favoured school, listed her special reasons, "I like to dress up in my uniform. Also, we go for picnics. Once, we went to India Gate and we had *bahut majja*, great fun.

Then there is morning assembly where we sing so many different songs." Her words set off a renewed wave of nostalgia for school. Priya said, "There are festival celebrations like Diwali *mela* (fair). Once, during Christmas, ma'am dressed up as Santa Claus!" Another child remembered the prizes they would get for doing something or other, "Little kits: doctor kit, cooking kit…" Sandeep cut in, "Now, with online classes, we get nothing." His particular favourite was the games period. Priya went on, "This time on August 15, ma'am gave us an assignment to make a project on Independence Day. I wanted to do it well but it was too difficult. If I was at school, I could have pleaded with ma'am for help!" The discussion then jumped to what they seemed to miss most of all: the midday meal. Items like "roti-chana" "rajma chawal" and "alu ki sabzi" were recalled, as also treats like "besan ka ladoo" and "kheer" on special days.

These young voices find an echo in a survey on school education, "Locked Out Emergency Report on School Education", released in early September 2021. Although the 1,400 school children that figured in this report came from rural backgrounds, what they had in common with their counterparts in the Delhi bastis were the remarkably similar forms of marginalisation they faced during the pandemic (Bakhla, et al., 2021). According to the survey's findings, only 8 per cent of the sample children were actually studying online regularly, while 37 per cent were not studying at all, and many—at least half the number surveyed—could not read more than a few words (ibid.). According to the study, apart from a small section of relatively better off children, the prospect of continued schooling had become more distant for the majority (ibid.). What also came through in the survey was that parents believed that, by and large, the capacity of their children to read and write had actually registered a decline during the pandemic (ibid.).

Similar sentiments were expressed by the mothers we met in the Delhi bastis. Each one of them was driven by the fierce determination to ensure that their children broke out of the endless cycle of poverty and hunger that had marked their own lives. When they were asked what they desired most of all from life, their answers were almost identical. Sushila, who lives in the Lal Gumbad camp, put it simply, "You see our lives. Our families face so many reversals. I don't want that to happen to our children. I want them to have a *sarkari naukri* (government job), so that they are guaranteed a stable life. But to get a *sarkari naukri*, they need to have a good education and that is our dearest wish."

Many of these women have laboured hard in the homes of the rich, washing dishes and swabbing floors until their hands have turned raw. In better times, some had even managed to save enough to put their children into a private school or arrange for tuition—an extra expense of at least Rs 300 a month for a child in a lower class. But with the COVID-19 virus, the fragile edifice of their dreams had collapsed. "The *mahamari* changed everything. Two lockdowns have upended our lives," said Putul, whose husband once had a good job in a textile export house. Today, both husband and wife scour their locality for odd jobs to earn a little cash; they feel crushed under a large debt burden.

Her son, Sandeep, who figured in the conversation cited earlier, demonstrated how he did his online class by perching his mobile phone on a water bottle. But Putul was unsure about how much he was actually learning. This is a doubt expressed by many mothers we spoke to, who felt intuitively that their children were losing out because of virtual classes, despite the enthusiastic claim of the Government of India's Ministry of Human Resource Development in its publicity material, that online learning was about "anytime, anywhere learning" (Government of India, n.d.).

Soni, who lives in Jagdamba Camp, was particularly worried about her 12-year-old daughter, Muskaan. "She is hyper-active and doesn't understand much although she pretends she does," she remarked, adding that she would have been happier if her daughter was in an *asli* (real) classroom with an *asli* teacher. During this period of two lockdowns, the children in the lower classes were

Putul with her son, Sandeep, and a neighbour's child. During the lockdown, Sandeep would attend his online class by perching the family cellphone on a water bottle.

promoted but that in no way reassured their parents. Poonam, the mother of Priya, one of the children quoted earlier, knows that her daughter is bright, which was why she and her husband put her in a private school in the neighbourhood, Vidya Bal Vihar, despite the additional expense. But now, even though Poonam is herself unlettered, she clearly perceived how disrupted her daughter's education had become.

Yashoda, of Lal Gumbad, came directly to the point, "In our home there is no smartphone so my eldest child, Sangeeta, who was in Class 4, cannot attend online classes. Despite this, she got promoted to the fifth last year, and now they are pushing her into the sixth. This worries me to no end. I don't know how she will manage. Already, she is forgetting whatever she had learnt. If we had money, I could have arranged for tuition, but now that is impossible." These are women who have themselves had to drop out of school for some reason or the other. In the case of Sushila, it was because her mother cut herself badly with a scythe while working in the fields, back home in a village in Rae Bareli district. This meant that Sushila, then in Class 8, had to give up her education and her ambition of becoming a policewoman.

The pandemic left these women as the sole supervisors of their children's education, a task that overwhelmed them. Sushila put it well, "Sometimes my children make my head spin—*dimaag kharab karte hain.* My son sees a lot of things on the net, I don't even know what he sees and that is a cause of concern for me."

The mobile phone became an absolute necessity at the very juncture that it had become unaffordable for most households. Children from families that didn't possess one were shut out of schooling by default. In Jagdamba Camp, Rani's grandchild, Kajal, and Nujita Bano's little boys, Mohammed Ayaan, 6, and Mohammad Rehan, 5, were among those thrown out. The latter two were enrolled in school but, as Nujita Bano pointed out, ever since she admitted them there has been a lockdown and since only their father had a cell phone, which he needed to access work, they have not been introduced to schooling of any kind as yet. The high cost of recharging also riled her, "The recharge always gets over, and for renewal we need at least Rs 350 for a 28-day package. When we don't have money to feed the children, from where do we get money for recharge?"

This was a familiar conundrum in these bastis. Chanchal's small room in the Lal Gumbad neighbourhood is often the scene of pitched battles for the one mobile phone the family has. "My three children, Suchetna, Sachin, and Shivam, have to share one cell phone for their studies, so they fight a lot for it. Just recharging costs us Rs 200 a month—but because the bandwidth is not adequate for Zoom, on which these classes are delivered, we had to spend up to Rs 600 for a plan of 48 to 56 days, something we can ill afford and which only adds to our debt," she said.

Private schools provided students with tablets (or "tabs", as they are called) but this, ironically, became yet another source of worry. Sushila explained, "We've put our children into a private school, Vidya Bal Vihar. My eldest boy, Dipanshu, sits for three-and-a-half hours at a stretch, attending his online classes. After the lockdown, the school sent us a tablet and the box it came in had the figure "Rs 16,000" written in big bold letters on it. We, as parents, had to give an undertaking that it will be returned to the school in perfect condition once their classrooms open. This makes my heart race. If something does happen to it—if it falls down and breaks, repaying the school for the tab will be impossible for us." As it was, admitting even one child to a private school had become prohibitive for the family, because fees of around Rs 150 per month could only be paid by raising loans. Her second son was born in 2016, and they have still not decided on his school. But the idea of sending one child to private school and the other to a government one didn't feel right to her.

Parents in the bastis, given precarious household finances, kept wrestling with these decisions throughout the pandemic. Many took the decision to shift their children from private schools to government ones. Data from the Directorate of Education, Delhi Government, reveals that some 0.16 million students moved from private to free government schools in Delhi for the year 2021–22, with the percentage of those in Classes 9 to 11 being disproportionately higher (Chettri, 2021).

The older children we spoke to communicated the frustration they felt over online teaching. Soni's daughter, Kushboo, a former student of Sarvodaya Kanya Vidyalaya in Malviya Nagar, managed to score 80 per cent in her Class 12 board examinations in 2021. When we met her, she was busy trying to get admitted into college, but what really depressed her was the certainty that she would have got better marks and improved her chances of securing a seat in a good college, if her last year of schooling had not been through the online mode. "It just isn't like a classroom. In a classroom the

Soni is a mother of five children. Her eldest daughter Kushboo, who completed her 12th board examinations through online classes and secured 80 per cent, holds up her marks sheet.

teacher stands in front of you, and *dimaag lagte hai*—your mind works. Inside our houses, there are so many distractions that it is difficult to concentrate. The camera on the phone used to make me feel anxious every time class started," she recalled.

Like Kushboo, there were innumerable teenagers in Delhi's bastis trying to cope with disrupted schooling against great odds. One of them is 12-year-old Pinky of Jagdamba Camp. She loves Maths, likes English and drawing, and wants to be a school teacher. Pinky had just shifted from a primary school run by the South Delhi Municipal Corporation to Class 6 in the Sarvodaya Kanya Vidyalaya nearby. When we met her, she had received her textbooks, but her greatest regret was that she had not attended her new school. Her online classes began at 10:00 a.m. and went on non-stop till 3:00 p.m. When we asked her how she managed to study in a noisy neighbourhood, she replied with composure, "I shut the door." Online classes are attended with Pinky sitting bolt upright on a large bed that she shares with her widowed mother; a bed that almost fills their one-room tenement. Her only complaint was that her shoulders ached by the time the classes wound down. Pinky, incidentally, also pitched in to assist her mother as a household help—the family's only source of income. Her mother's health had been poor of late, and that meant that Pinky often had to accompany her mother to the homes of her employers to clean floors while the latter did the dishes.

The crucial role of schooling in keeping children from joining the labour market or from being forced into early marriages is well understood. In a November 2020 report, UNICEF noted that many, among the 247 million children enrolled in an estimated 1.5 million elementary and secondary schools in India which shut down during the pandemic, were at risk of "slipping into child

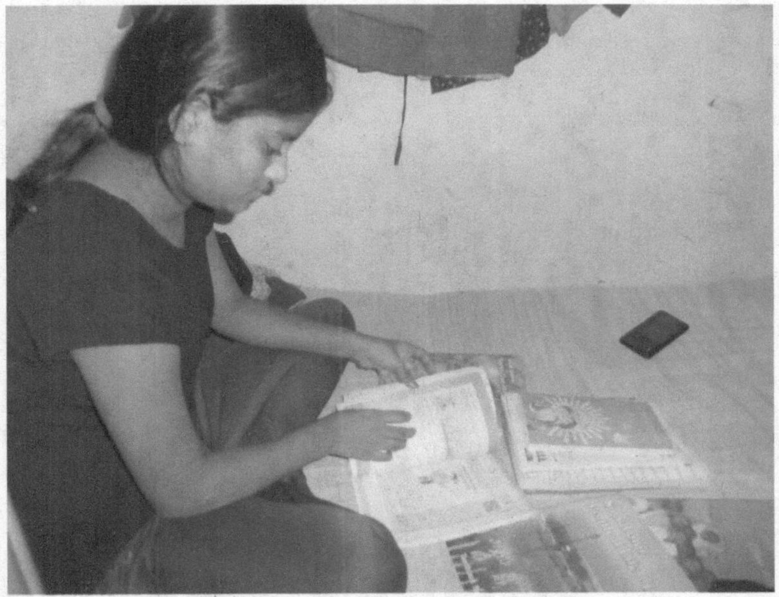

Pinky, 12, in the one-room tenement she shares with her mother, attended online classes from 10 a.m. to 3 p.m. during the pandemic. Her only complaint was that her shoulders always ached at the end of the class.

labour and unsafe migration"(PTI, 2021). Similarly, going by distress calls received by CHILDLINE India Foundation, a nodal agency of the Union Ministry of Women and Child Development, there was a rising trend of parents forcing their wards into early marriages (Jejeebhoy, 2021).

In our conversations with families living in Delhi's bastis, we could sense that a tipping point was imminent in some instances. No one wanted their children to start working, but the fact was that many youngsters were already earning some money for the family by helping out in a shop or operating a cycle rickshaw. Parents of daughters on the verge of turning 18 may also have been mulling over the possibility of marriage for them although in the pre-pandemic days, they would have been far more open to the idea of allowing their teenagers to study a little further. One mother in the basti we talked to, in fact, told us that she was waiting for

A typical scene during the pandemic. With schools closed, the children spent their time as best as they could.

her 17-year-old daughter, whom she had sent back to the village, to turn 18 before considering a match for her. The inexorable logic of a deepening pandemic-driven poverty is threatening to drown out those chirpy, young voices we heard speaking of their experiences of schooling with so much enthusiasm and excitement.

Chapter 6
The Disabled Got Left Behind

The first lockdown, once it was announced on March 25, 2020, was presumed to be a brief period of inconvenience. But with every day that it dragged on, the impact on India's poorest and most vulnerable groups began to be perceived. We saw how joblessness and homelessness forced migrant workers to walk down highways on the long journey back to their villages and towns. Quickly made apparent as well, were the consequences that home quarantining had on couples confined within the home, and the way this led to a significant rise in cases of domestic violence. The grave loss of school learning because classrooms had now turned virtual also became a subject of public conversations. But among the least articulated issues was the way the pandemic greatly added to the disabilities of the differently-abled.

It took a while for this reality to be understood, even for those who have been working closely with the community. Binod Kumar, programme manager of Astha, an organisation that has been focusing on children and persons with disabilities since 1993, remarked, "For the disabled, particularly those living in the bastis, the pandemic had double the implications and proved a major challenge." With his office adjoining the Govindpuri basti, Kumar slowly came to understand first-hand the calamitous consequences the pandemic had for the poorest families who had members living with disability.

With no money at hand and confined to their homes, these families could not access the medicines needed for those with special needs. There were those, for instance, in urgent need of anti-epileptic drugs to control seizures, but who just could not procure them. Astha, with its master-list of about 2,000 families living in the surrounding bastis with disabled children or family members, tried to respond to the crisis by linking up with nearby chemists and getting them to drop off essential medicines to isolated families. But the great number of basti-dwellers and their far flung locations resulted in many being left out of such networks, and many who had to handle the health emergencies they faced as best as they could.

"Isolation only adds to general distress, and counselling becomes crucial in situations like this. We did what little we could. I remember receiving calls of distress even from homeless families living under flyovers. One disabled woman told us over the phone that she could not cope with her situation and felt there was no way out for her but to commit suicide, so great was her helplessness," recalled Kumar.

The few support structures that do exist for the community, like schools for children with special needs, were shut down during this period. As a result, parents of disabled children, mothers especially, had to look after their children 24x7. It made for an impossible situation to have to manage a disabled child in need of special care at a time when the family itself was in a state of mental panic, with no sources of income, and hunger staring them in the face. Kumar was informed by many mothers about how they had stood in lines for 12 hours to get some food and had to sometimes return to their hungry children empty-handed. Aditi Dwivedi, of SNS, also pointed out how dietary supplements made available through schemes like the Pradhan Mantri Matru Vandana Yojana, even if it reached the family, was denied to the third child.

Situations of hunger and impoverishment have the potential of leading to breakdown and abuse. Kumar revealed, "The threshold of family tension rises exponentially if a family member or a child is disabled. *Maar-peet shuru ho jaata hain* (beatings begin); in some instance even the disabled child gets thrashed."

We visited the home of Neelu, 17, a patient of cerebral palsy, who lives in a one-room tenement in the Govindpuri basti with her mother and brother. Her mother explained how Neelu was born a healthy baby but later contracted a fever and was never the same again. The child's limbs didn't seem to work properly—that was the first thing that struck the mother. It was only later that a doctor diagnosed her condition as cerebral palsy and assured the mother that the child would get better as she grew up. His diagnosis proved right—Neelu learnt with great difficulty to survive. She attended a government school until she reached a point when she could no longer cope with the lessons.

The lockdown saw that tenuous link she had with schooling finally snap. She was in Class 9, when she dropped out in 2020. Class 9, incidentally, is a stage when many so-called underperformers are forced out of the schooling system. Neelu told us clearly how she felt about this, "I want to feel happy. I kept thinking to myself, 'why is it that I cannot do what the other kids are doing?' They would be after me, calling me a *buddhu* (dunce), and it made me feel very sad. I would long for a friend who would come to school with me and eat with me."

The end of schooling for her brought relief in some senses, as it spared her from being teased by classmates, but the lockdown affected her adversely as well, "I felt agitated and wondered where we could go, and how we would live. I saw my ammi's distress, and that would lead to all kinds of worries in my head."

A major problem that many families of disabled children faced during the pandemic was immense difficulty in procuring an extremely vital document: the Certificate of Disability. This certification is mandatory for everything, whether it is to get into a school or access health care. To acquire it the family would need a birth certificate, an Aadhaar card, and the Aadhaar cards of the

Neelu, 17, a patient of cerebral palsy, was forced to drop out of school during the first wave of the pandemic.

parents—all of which would have to provide proof that the family had been living in Delhi for at least the last five years.

Earlier, procuring such a certificate was relatively easy. The child was taken to the Outpatient Department (OPD) of a public hospital and examined by a trained doctor. A form had to be filled and submitted. Generally within a fortnight, a specially constituted Board would examine the child and the disability certificate would reach the family within the next six weeks or so.

Everything became far more complex during the pandemic, with parents being given the runaround, constantly instructed to contact one office or the other. Kumar explained their trauma, "Under lockdown, nothing moved, and all the institutional energy seemed to be focused on COVID-19. Everything was now online, and for people who had no cell phones, things became impossible. We tried to raise awareness and information in the community on how to procure certificates online. To get one appointment online, our staff would spend two or three days and even after that the certificate would not reach." It was a similar process to access a disability pension that a person becomes entitled to if they have at least 40 per cent disability.

A sensitive issue that remains largely hidden, was the risk of being sexually attacked by vagabonds that young people with disability faced—a situation common during the pandemic. Arti, a special educator, explained that if a disabled person happens to be a girl, she is doubly at risk of such assault. She explained, "Disabled kids often do not sense when they should keep a distance from someone. They hug everyone, approach everyone in a friendly way and sometimes are cruelly taken advantage of."

She cites two cases that came up during this period. One involved a family where all the members were equally disabled and communicated only through sign language. Their young daughter was raped by either their landlord or his son. The incident was so disturbing for the family that they didn't even want to file a case. The other instance involved an assault on a 14-year-old. Her caregiver—who happened to be her grandmother—had the presence of mind to quickly file a police complaint, and justice could be sought in that case.

Trainers like Arti attempt to impart information on adolescence, gender, and sexuality to children with disability, "We talk about sexuality to both parents and the child. We tell kids about 'good touch', 'bad touch'." These are important initiatives, but self-protection is hard for those who find it difficult to express themselves, who cannot see or whose locomotor system is impaired in some way.

The lack of access to regular hospital check-ups for pregnant women during the pandemic also raised concerns in this context—monitoring for the first signs of disability in the foetus had now become impossible. Kumar pointed out, "If the expectant mother is malnourished and under stress, it could have severe repercussions on the baby she is carrying. The pandemic was a period when thousands upon thousands of medically unmonitored women were not getting adequate nutrition and had to cope with extremely high levels of tension within the household. We learnt that many women ended up delivering breech babies because their pre-delivery consultations could not take place. Such babies could suffer from disabilities later in life."

Checking the developmental milestones of the baby, once it was born, could also not be done satisfactorily because that required regular physical consultations. During the pandemic period, all monitoring had to be done virtually. That premature babies would be born to families bereft of any support during this period was a lurking worry for disability activists like Kumar. As he put it, "To address disability, the earlier the intervention, the better the prognosis—we have had children who showed signs of disability in infanthood and went on to lead perfectly normal lives because they were given adequate attention. But such interventions came to a standstill during the pandemic."

The experience of Ajay Saxena, who once ran a flourishing hardware enterprise, demonstrated the crucial importance of early medical attention. His son, Rahul (name changed), now 11, was a baby who didn't speak at two years like most toddlers. "When he was two and a half, we started approaching doctors and even visited the All India Institute of Medical Sciences. The diagnosis at that time was that he was suffering from a hearing disorder. It was only later that we were told that our son was showing signs of autism. Today, Rahul does speak and can inform us of what he wants. But if he had proper medical attention earlier, things would have been far, far better," said his father.

Saxena does not live in a basti. In fact he has his own home in Kalkaji, a middle-class neighbourhood close to the Govindpuri basti, but he has been living on the verge of bankruptcy for some time now. He put it this way, "There was a time when I was a prosperous man with a thriving hardware enterprise. After the market collapsed during the first lockdown, I had to sell off my assets to try and recover some of the losses. My business started failing just before the lockdown and it collapsed as a result of the lockdown. We also didn't imagine that the first lockdown would go on for 68 days. I used to make some extra money renting out my two extra rooms to young office goers. The lockdown meant that even that source of income disappeared. Today, I have a debt touching Rs 5 lakh."

All this took a grave toll on Saxena's health; he was diagnosed with a serious heart condition, but given his precarious financial condition, he has indefinitely postponed the surgery he requires.

Despite his own failing health, what he is constantly preoccupied by is the well-being and future of his only son. "There have been times when Rahul has been called 'abnormal' to his face. This hurts me like anything. He is not abnormal, he is just a kid with a communicating disability," said Saxena. He knows that his son needs to run around and play with other children, but that became impossible during the lockdown period, when he had to be confined within the home and denied even small pleasures like the occasional ice cream.

Ajay's wife added, "Mummy *ke saat rahete hain* (he stays with me all the time) and that's not good. The main problem is that he has no friends, and even when he tries to show affection to young children, they feel he has come to attack them. They don't understand him. The lockdown has made things worse because it has ended any opportunity he may have had to interact with other children."

Taking care of children with special needs proved to be a major challenge for mothers in the basti during the pandemic.

Rahul attends a local school and even does his homework conducted online through worksheets. On the wish list of both parents are speech therapy classes for their son. But this would cost something like Rs 8,000 every month, something they can ill afford, given their present financial situation. Their biggest desire is for Rahul to learn to speak properly so that he can lead an independent life in the future, when they both may no longer be around to support him.

Chapter 7

When the Roof Goes, the Foundation of Life Disintegrates

Many in the homeless shelters of Delhi have personal experiences of their homes being razed before their eyes. They carry with them shard-like memories of police lathis being used against them, bulldozers and rising mounds of rubble. The great irony was that even as people were told to keep themselves safe by staying within their homes during the pandemic, the roofs of hundreds of thousands of Delhi residents were brought crashing down through demolition drives during this period.

Kalyani Menon-Sen, who co-authored the book, *Swept off the Map: Surviving Eviction and Resettlement in Delhi*, points out that in April 2020, the UN Rapporteur on The Right to Housing had called for a moratorium on evictions during the lockdown (United Nations Human Rights Office of the High Commissioner, n.d.). "Some countries may have heeded this call, but not India. Here, the lockdown was an opportunity for the state to go ahead with 'clean up operations'. In Delhi, at the peak of the second wave, the Municipal Corporation, the Railways, the DDA, the Forest Department, demolished the settlements they had on their lists, without notice and without mercy. Such drives were common in an earlier time as well, but the pandemic period was seized as an opportunity to clear hutments quickly with no pesky activists blocking the bulldozers, mobilising the media, or running to the courts," observed Menon-Sen in a conversation with us.

Neelesh Kumar, of the Basti Surakhsha Manch, estimated that the period of the pandemic from the first lockdown onwards saw demolitions occurring in at least 13 locations in Delhi with at least 1,100 homes in bastis being flattened, impacting over 7,000 people. According to data from the Housing and Land Rights Network (HLRN), during the pandemic, the authorities demolished 43,000 homes and evicted 250,000 across the country (Chaudhry, et al., 2021). Nearly 16 million faced displacement, which included the two million whose claims to forest land stood rejected.

Being destroyed were not just buildings, but people's lives and sense of themselves as human beings. In a Nizamuddin *rain basera* (or common shelter for the city's homeless), we came across 22-year-old Sameena. Originally from Madhubani, Bihar, she grew up in a basti near the Nizamuddin *nullah* (drain). Life took her to many pockets of the country: she worked as a child labourer in a Bhiwandi powerloom unit; as a house maid to a family in Kashmir; and later, as a caretaker of children in a household in Delhi's upscale neighbourhood of Jangpura. She would have liked to have continued working there, but her employer got cold feet, since Sameena looked very young. Said Sameena, "My *memsahib* helped me get an Aadhaar card for which I will always be grateful to her. But one day she called me aside and said, 'The government is getting strict about the employment of under-age workers in homes, so you will have to leave.'"

This step left Sameena extremely vulnerable. An 18-year-old man who was working as an attendant in a guest house in the neighbourhood came into her life, promising to marry her. Before a marriage could take place, she became pregnant with her first-born. A few months after her first child was born, she was pregnant with a second child.

Around the first week of April 2020, the Tablighi Jamaat, a Sunni Muslim organisation, organised an event in its Nizamuddin headquarters, which was quickly framed by the authorities and the media as a "super spreader" event (IANS, 2020). This led to the entire area being deemed a "Corona virus hotspot" (Pradhan, Trivedi and Bloomberg, 2020). The police blindly rounded up the residents of the Nizamuddin basti area where Sameena now lived. She recalled that moment, "I was breastfeeding my older son, and was pregnant with my younger one, when the police pushed us into a bus and dumped us in a school in the Sarai Kale Khan area." Sameena and some other women in the group made a huge ruckus. One of them had a mobile phone and they made a video to prove that they were starving, thirsty and had been taken to an unknown place. The police, probably intimidated by this move, freed them after a few days, and Sameena found her way to the *shamshan ghat* (crematorium) at Jangpura, an area she was familiar with. "It was hot and miserable. I was itching all over, I remember how I wanted to scratch the skin off of my body. When any policeman came near me I would scream, 'I have a child in my stomach, don't trouble me'."

A couple of months later she gave birth to her second child on the street, with the help of a local *baba* (local holy man) and a *dai* (midwife) who lived in the area. They ensured that she was admitted to hospital, and was given her shots and some rudimentary care. Today, as Sameena carries her two babies wherever she goes, she makes a pale anaemic figure—the lack of health care during her pregnancies shows. Clearly the rough experiences of homelessness have taken an enormous toll on her physical well-being. If it were not for the free food that people were distributing on the streets in those days, she and her two babies would have starved. She said, "That was a time when people would distribute rice meals, biscuits and milk in the area. We could live because of the kindness of strangers whom I will always regard as *farishtas* (angels)."

Today, Sameena lives in the *rain basera* and earns for her two children—one a babe in arms, the other a toddler—by begging on

Both of Sameena's children were born on the street during the pandemic (she is seen here with her elder one). The toll that child birth, homelessness, and poor nutrition took on her during this difficult time, shows on her face.

the streets. "We are lucky to get some space here in this shelter. Life is hell on the streets. I remember once, I managed to procure a piece of tarpaulin sheet from a dump yard and used it to cover a part of the pavement where my child lay. One afternoon, a storm raged and the tarpaulin got blown away. How bitterly I cried over that!"

Today, her children have a solid roof above their heads, and two meals a day distributed in the shelter around midday and in the late evening. But to ensure that they survive, she knows she must keep earning, "I leave my things here in the shelter and go out to beg. I sit on the pavement keeping one child in my lap and holding the other. When passers-by see me they have different reactions. Many signal their contempt at being asked for alms and even push me away, but there are people—pedestrians and motorists—who feel pity and drop something for me—a five or ten rupee coin, and occasionally even a 100 or 500 rupee note. Often, they fling the money at me, as if I am dirt. This hurts me deeply, but I am grateful for whatever comes my way."

During the pandemic, she was often instructed to wear a mask by strangers on the street but observed that she had never been afraid of the *mahamari*, only of the police and the street mafia, "There are people out there who want to drag and assault me or ask me whether I will go with them. So I take care to wear dirty clothes, walk without sandals, and cover my head with a dirty piece of cloth when I go to beg. If someone comes after me despite all this and misbehaves, I know how to scream, and there are many on the streets who recognise me and will not hesitate to protect me."

Sameena's account indicates how, when the roof goes, the foundation of life disintegrates. Ruby, 40, another resident in the Nizamuddin *rain basera*, has had similar experiences. Now a divorcee, she was married twice. Both men turned out to be drunkards and drug addicts. Ruby joined the ranks of the homeless after the basti she lived in, in the Amir Khusrao Park area near the Nizamuddin dargah, was set on fire and razed to the ground in 2017. It was home to over 200 largely Muslim families working as labourers, hawkers, and people who begged for a living.

Mother of three, Ruby, another resident of the homeless shelter, lost her job during the lockdown. Her big dream is to set up a home outside the shelter so that her daughter's groom, when she gets married, doesn't have to know that she is homeless.

"From having a roof, we suddenly went to having nothing. Everything either went up in flames or was reduced to rubble. Living in the open without any protection was frightening," Ruby told us. It is not just the rodents and dogs that she was scared of, her biggest fear was that her children—Saiba, Shabana, and Farhan, now 16, 13 and 8 respectively—would be snatched away from her. From those days, she has developed the habit of falling asleep only in the early hours of the day in order to keep an eye on her sleeping children throughout the night.

The pandemic saw her ability to earn come to an abrupt end. "When the *mahamari* came and with it the lockdown—it was around the time of Ramzan—they did not allow us to leave the *rain basera* and locked us in. I couldn't go out and earn the Rs 4,000 or 5,000 I used to make by working in people's homes. When I went back after the first lockdown was lifted, my *memsahibs* had found other help and I lost my sources of livelihood," she revealed.

Ruby looks malnourished. Her mouth is discoloured from chewing *paan* and she complains of menstrual problems. She worries that the calcium from her bones is seeping out of her, but her greatest anxiety is related to getting some work to ensure that her children are spared the indignities she has had to suffer. She would like to have a room to call her own rather than live eternally in a homeless shelter. "My elder daughter will soon be of marriageable age. How can my *damaad* (future son-in-law) come and visit us in this *rain basera*?" she asked dejectedly.

The supervisor of this homeless shelter, Radha, understands only too well the experiences of women like Sameena and Ruby; she too has lived on the streets, growing up as a child near Delhi's Kalkaji Mandir and having been trafficked at an early age. "To live on the streets as a woman is to expose yourself and your body to the most demonic forces on earth. Who am I to regard these women as outcasts? I have also gone through the experiences they have. Demolitions during Corona *kaal* (times) have only increased their numbers," she said.

One of the sites where the bulldozers have been at work is Khori Gaon that lies on the border of Delhi and Haryana. Neelesh Kumar's Basti Surakhsha Manch is among the organisations working to help the displaced community there. "This clearance drive had pre-dated the pandemic, but in June 2021, at the height of the monsoon, things came to a head when the Supreme Court ordered the removal of all encroachments on forest land in the area. Within hours of this, the police landed up there and started pasting notices of imminent demolition."

Who are these basti-dwellers? They originally worked at the mines that were operating in the area. The local mafia had offered them land at dirt-cheap rates. In order to procure it and secure a foothold in the city for their children, people put together their entire savings, sold the small holdings and assets they had back in the village, and bought the plots. Today, the homes they struggled to build over the years have been reduced to broken bricks, and the land has slipped away from under their feet. Any hope of rehabilitation rested on documents like electricity bills and ration cards which most families did not possess.

Kumar had innumerable stories of distress to narrate about the repression meted out by the police and the helplessness of the Khori Gaon basti-dweller. "There was this pregnant woman who saw her house being demolished before her eyes and fainted. She just lay there, and I heard police personnel say, 'Let her die'."

The fate of Khori Gaon's residents could be that of people living in any of the unauthorised bastis of Delhi at any time. According to Kumar, houses are already being broken down without any notice being issued to the residents of Delhi's Sangam Vihar. The homeless have shared their desperate isolation with Kumar, "People tell me that losing a home is like losing one's eldest son—with the house goes their lives and future. After all, why do people come to the big city? They come in the hope of a little shelter under which they could build their own lives and that of their children. They invest so much effort in trying to achieve this."

Years ago, Jean Dreze, an economist, and Bela Bhatia, a sociologist, writing in the context of Delhi's bastis, argued that the notion that slums were parasitical settlements that tarnished the urban environment—an argument often used to justify demolitions—overlooked their essential economic purpose (HT Correspondent, 2007). They provide low-cost housing to masses of workers who "service" the city, and for whom no provision was made in urban development planning (ibid.).

Neelesh Kumar reiterated this. "Can you imagine Delhi without the people who built it? Can any city survive without the labour of the men and women who live in almost unseen pockets of the city? Those who have money and have built palaces on forest land illegally have escaped, unhurt, while these impoverished families are being rendered invisible, jobless, and homeless so that Delhi can be "beautified". Is this the way we reciprocate their efforts in building the city's infrastructure and wealth through their labour?" he asked.

Chapter 8

To Be Old, Crippled and Alone
is to Experience a Lockdown of Life

"I came to this city as a young woman. Now I am old." That was how Rani, who lives in a two-room unit in Jagdamba Camp basti, summed up her life. She doesn't know her precise age, but she could be in her late sixties. Her emaciated limbs testify to decades of undernutrition. She complained that her feet have now started hurting a lot when she walks, and sometimes her mind just doesn't work, "*mera dimaag chalta nahin*".

To listen to her life story is to understand how a metropolis like Delhi can consume the youth and energies of millions like Rani, and leave them severely alone in a time like a pandemic, when they are in urgent need of support.

Rani came from the village of Gadha Garhi in Uttar Pradesh's Agra district. At 13, she married a man far older to her, and the only thing she had to say about him was that he was not unkind to her. She followed him to the sprawling shanty town of Jagdamba Camp, which proliferated over a sewer line in the Delhi colony of Sheikh Sarai. Both husband and wife settled to a hardscrabble existence. He worked as a *safai karamchari* in two or three hospitals, while she worked in people's homes, washing their dishes and mopping their floors. Together they earned enough to actually buy a couple of rooms in Jagdamba Camp over time. This made Rani one of those rare women we met in these bastis who was not a *kirayadaar* (tenant). Not having to pay rent was a huge relief, but there is a story here as well, to which we will come back later.

The days passed. The couple had children and these children in turn grew up, got married, and had children of their own. One daughter settled elsewhere after her marriage. Another daughter, Kiran, was lost to typhoid. Rani's son got married, became a father of 2, and then— about six years ago—suddenly contracted a fever and died. That death proved to be a tipping point in her life because it meant that she, now in her late middle-age, would have to be a parent all over again. "My daughter-in-law just handed their two children to me and said that she couldn't take care of them. At that time their son, Kunal, was about 7, and daughter, Kajol, a few weeks old and as big as my forearm," Rani recalled.

A year later, Rani's husband died—again, a victim of *"bukhar"*, a fever. She was now left with the responsibility of bringing up her two grandchildren on her own.

"After my husband died, I felt grief-stricken and frightened. Some neighbours—*dabang log hain* (they were local thugs)—then turned up and said that since her husband owed them money, they were going to take over the house," revealed Rani. They captured one room and swore that they would take the rest of her property after her death.

"So far they have not beaten me, but they have informed me in no uncertain terms that they will throw my grandchildren out once I die," Rani revealed. Although she spoke with a calm expression, the words that followed expressed her sense of dread, "I feel that my life is being robbed from me."

She did not have even a sheet of paper to claim ownership of the property. In fact, apart from her Aadhaar card, she had no documents, and the people who were claiming ownership of the room made sure that she didn't get an electricity bill.

"I know how to struggle. Despite my years, I still used to do several jobs in people's homes, each paying anything from

Rs 600 to Rs 800, so that my grandchildren could eat. But the pandemic ended my working life, leaving me feeling old and useless," Rani explained. On the first day after the first lockdown was announced, her employers, one after the other, told her that she was too infirm to work in their homes, and that in any case, they cannot allow her into their houses and allow her to touch their vessels because of the *mahamari*. She then realised that her struggle to remain in the workforce had come to an end permanently.

That was how she found herself without any source of livelihood in the middle of a raging pandemic. Although entitled to an old age pension of Rs 2,500 provided by the Delhi government, Rani did not have any of the documents needed to access it: no singly-operated account in any bank, no proof that she has been a Delhi resident for five years, no caste certificate. She did not even have a mobile phone.

As the chokehold of the pandemic tightened around the family, her grandson Kunal—now about 14—joined the workforce. He got himself a rickshaw by taking a loan of Rs 150, which he still has to pay back. He used it to transport small items, but since this did not bring in any significant returns, he gave up on the idea and shifted to a job as a cleaner in an establishment in the neighbouring Savitri Nagar. On the day we visited their home, even that job was not there. Kunal had no employment to speak of, although he kept trying to do odd jobs. He was an adolescent, but had the bearing of an adult, and like a grown man, he was proud and didn't reveal that he was hungry and confused. His grandmother knew that he often went to bed without having eaten. It pained her but there was little she could do since that was also her lot. "This is the time for children to study and I feel very sad that my grandchildren are not in school," she stated. Although both children were born in Delhi, Rani did not have their birth certificates, and the granddaughter, Kajol, who was around 6, had not yet been enrolled in school.

Rani with her grandson, Kunal, 15, whom she brought up after his father died. During the lockdown, Kunal joined the workforce at 14, plying a rickshaw to transport material, thus losing out on schooling.

In many ways, Rani depended on the kindness of the people around her. "If someone from the neighbourhood gives me *sabzi*, I keep it for the children. Sometimes they give me *chaas* (buttermilk). Meals for us are mostly *kali chai* (black tea) and a *roti*, or some *chawal*." Her grandchildren love her and sometimes sleep by her side, creating rare moments of happiness in a life whittled down to the bone.

Rani's lack of a mobile phone highlights a situation common to many elderly people we met in Delhi's bastis and homeless shelters. The biggest challenge faced by them, according to data put out by HelpAge India, was in "accessing healthcare, buying medicines, groceries and banking" (HelpAge India, 2020). With the pandemic, services of this kind migrated to the virtual mode at an accelerated pace and most of the elderly poor found technology a bridge too far to cross. The post-3G generation—those born in the twenty-first century—could make the transition to the online mode relatively easily, so even the realisation of the deeply disempowering impacts of tech-centred solutions was lost on the general population and on policy makers in particular. Media scholars term this the "grey digital divide" (Huxhold, Hees and Webster, 2020), which only keeps expanding with ever-growing technologies flooding the market.

The case of 79-year-old Devki bai, living alone in Motilal Nehru camp near Munirka, illustrated this poignantly. She made a frail figure, with a severe stoop after an accident, when a log of wood fell on her. Her greatest support had been a ration card that bore her name. In July 2020, with much difficulty and after spending money on an autorickshaw, she made it to the ration shop. It proved to be a wasted trip. Her fingerprints did not match the records in the electronic Point of Scale (e-POS) device yet again. This was an old problem for her. In 2018, when the e-POS with Aadhaar-based biometric authentication was introduced on a trial basis, it was discovered that the machine could not read her fingerprints, which had been effaced by her advanced years and a lifetime of hard work.

For elderly women like Devki bai, there was the additional problem of ration shops being shut or functioning only for limited hours during the lockdowns in many parts of the city. In a survey conducted right after the first lockdown was announced, a team from Delhi Rozi Roti Adhikar Abhiyan (DRRAA), a network of groups working on food security, which includes Satark Nagrik Sangathan (SNS), found that 13 out of the 37 ration shops it had visited were shut most of the time (Staff Reporter 2020). Campaigns and public hearings conducted by the DRRAA and the RTI queries filed have finally forced the Food and Civil Supplies Department of the Delhi government to review this system of distribution. An August 2021 order specified that all Public Distribution System (PDS) beneficiaries above 65 or below 16, as well as families of the differently abled, can designate a relative or friend to collect their foodgrain entitlements for them (Burman, 2021).

Only time will tell how the new system will turn out. However, there was one aspect of a technology-driven life in socially distanced times that did not have an easy resolution: the loneliness and isolation brought about by the lack of a cell phone or the inability to use one because of trembling limbs and fading eyesight. While the rest of the world got in touch with friends and relatives virtually and through online events during the pandemic, here was a section left behind without the means to reach out to others. This also made them extremely vulnerable to crime and violence since they could not convey information about such occurrences to others and thus ensure swift action. According to a survey of 5,000 elderly people from different parts of India conducted by Agewell Foundation, every third elderly person had suffered some form of abuse during the lockdown period (World Elder Abuse Awareness Day, 15th June, 2021, Humans Rights of elderly are at stake, n.d.). The likelihood that they may also have lacked communication tools like mobile phones could well be a factor in the proliferation of such crimes.

In a homeless shelter at Yamuna Pushta, we met Ashok Kumar, a widower and former resident of Rajpur, a town in Patiala district. Now in his late 60s, he was once a person of modest means, with a house, a bank account and a small business. The pandemic saw the unravelling of his settled existence.

"I sold towels and jackets, and after paying for all the expenses, I would make about Rs 300-400 a day. Once the lockdown was announced, all the shops that stocked my goods in Panipat closed down. The items I had in stock got soiled and I had to give them away or discard them. The *mahamari* literally pushed me into the dust," Ashok Kumar recalled, his eyes moist.

Once the towel business collapsed, Ashok took to selling vegetables, but found that paying off the police each time meant he just could not break even. He then tried his hand at operating an e-rickshaw, but that failed as well. The house he once possessed had already been sold and he suspects that the property agent swindled him of a lion's share of the proceeds. The two lakh he received from that sale has been spent to settle his daughter's marriage. She now lives in Kurukshetra, and he had a plan to visit her, but emphatically stated that he will never live in her home because "parents don't live in their daughter's place—that is not in our culture."

Completely pauperised, Ashok Kumar decided to move out of Rajpur so that he would not be recognised and pitied by people known to him. He began to wander from place to place, living in temples and gurudwaras where he could access free food. But living rough extracted a huge price in terms of health and well-being. He removed his spectacle to show us his clouded eyes, "Without these glasses, I can see nothing. My constant anxiety is that they will get stolen or broken."

The anxiety was well-founded. Once, when he had sought shelter at the Old Delhi railway station, he was robbed of his phone. That loss has snapped the last link he had with the world he had

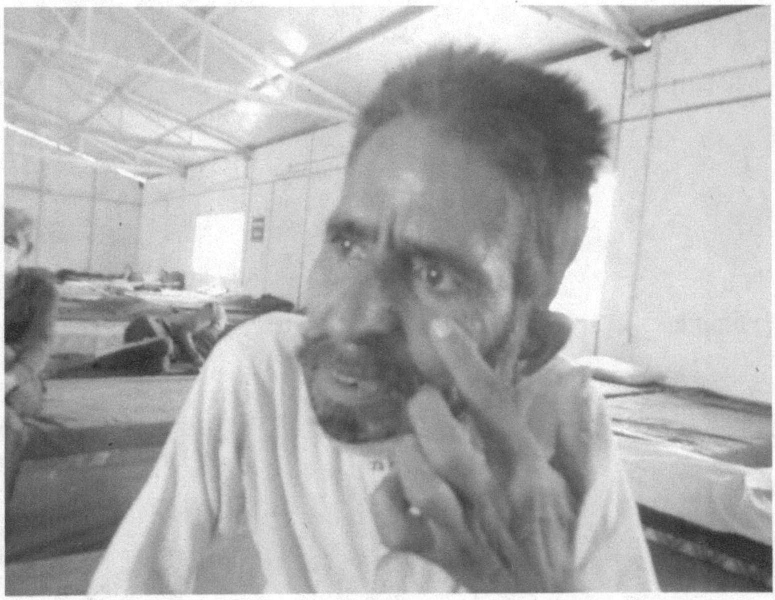

Ashok Kumar, a homeless widower, pointed to his clouded eyes. He lost his cellphone while taking shelter in a railway station during the lockdown. Now, his biggest fear is losing his spectacles because without them he is blind.

left behind. Today, he does not remember the numbers of his family members and contacts, and there is no way for his daughter to get in touch with him. Ashok Kumar intuitively understands that he has lost his sense of personhood, and there is little he can do about it, locked down as is in his own isolation, like so many other elderly people in the bastis and homeless shelters of Delhi.

Chapter 9
Health Emergencies:
Empty Purses and Mounting Debt

Long before the COVID-19 pandemic hit India, healthcare has been the single biggest factor for indebtedness among the poor. The pandemic only accelerated this trend. By June 2020 a couple of months after the March lockdown, it was found that individual income had dropped by nearly 40 per cent (Dhingra and Ghatak, 2021). But should that individual have happened to live in a basti and face illnesses, accidents and childbirth, the percentage of this decline would have been much higher.

Conversations we had with the residents of Delhi's bastis underlined this. Of course, a COVID-19 outbreak in a vulnerable family can set it back by huge amounts (and we have in this series an instance of that). According to research conducted by the Public Health Foundation of India and Duke Global Health Institute, the cost of ICU hospitalisation for COVID-19 in India is estimated to equal nearly 16 months of work for an ordinary worker (Gile, 2021). The point to note, however, is this: even if a family were to escape the fate of contracting the virus—and many in the bastis have had at least one dose of the vaccine, and that has helped protect them from the disease—even an affliction of less seriousness like a fall or a fever comes at an unaffordable cost at a time when purses are empty, debt is already mounting and opportunities to earn a sustainable livelihood are extremely uncertain.

When we met Sushila in the Lal Gumbad basti, she was suffering from a low-grade fever, which she said was affecting her entire family. "My husband had it, and then my two young sons fell ill. Today, I am feeling feverish. It does not seem to be Corona but I still worry. Generally, I try to take my children to the *mohalla* (neighbourhood) clinic or government hospital at least when they get a fever. The trouble is that we have to stand in long lines there to get our turn. Then the doctors are so distracted by the crowds that they barely ask you what the problem is. They examine us so hurriedly and scribble something so quickly that even before we can explain our condition properly, we are bundled out. Then we have to wait with another crowd in another queue outside the counter where they give out medicines. One feels that even if one is slightly sick, one will get seriously ill after going through all this. I suppose you can't blame these doctors and attendants, given the number of people who turn up, but somehow you lose hope in the system. Also, the medicines they give us never seem to help," she revealed.

It was this crisis of confidence in the public healthcare system that drove people to opt for self-medication or buy the drugs recommended by the chemist. If those didn't work, they desperately scrambled for the resources needed to access private healthcare. Take Sushila's argument, "When things don't get better we go for 'private'. We have more trust in the local Bengali doctor, who charges Rs 150 per visit and provides pills, than a government hospital. At least he listens to what our problem is, and tries to do something about it."

Incidentally, the colloquial term "Bengali doctor" in the basti refers to private medical practitioners, many of whom may not have an MBBS degree but have been able to run a successful practice catering to the local community. General private healthcare, despite the expense entailed, enjoys far greater credibility in the basti, lending credence to the conclusion reached in several surveys that in India, the private healthcare sector accounts for over 60 per cent of total out-of-pocket spending on health (Anand and Thampi, 2020). This is among the highest in the world.

The geography of the bastis, located as they are in the most marginalised, undesired and under-serviced areas of the national capital—near sewer lines and open drains; landfills and marshy spaces—also meant that their residents were constantly threatened by diseases caused by the unhygienic environment. These were also potential sites for serious calamities. For example, when a section of the Bhalswa landfill in northwest Delhi collapsed in August 2021, it led to several tenements in the vicinity being damaged, with residents being physically inundated by toxic waste.

The dangers inherent in the landscape were mirrored in the vulnerabilities within the bastis themselves, with their unplastered homes piled high, one upon the other, accessed only through steep, unsafe stairways. Nujita Bano's tiny room on the second floor in Jagdamba Camp houses herself, her husband, as well as three children, all below 6. Knowing how dangerous the staircase is, she tries to keep an eye out for her little ones as they run around and play. But she has not always been successful. When her eldest—Mohammed Ayaan, now 6—was an active toddler, he had slipped and rolled down two sets of stairs. He survived because he did not fall over the exposed side of the stairs where there was no handrail.

Earlier in 2021, after the second lockdown, her daughter Needa Parveen who is not yet 2, banged her head hard against the concrete corner of a stairway. Her mother recalled, "She was playing on the landing with another child when I heard her cry. I was cooking and did not immediately rush to find out what the matter was. I yelled at her, saying, 'Good, you have hurt yourself. Now you will learn your lesson. How many times have I told you not to go near the stairs?' But something in the nature of the child's shrill cries made me leave everything and rush to her side. I found her

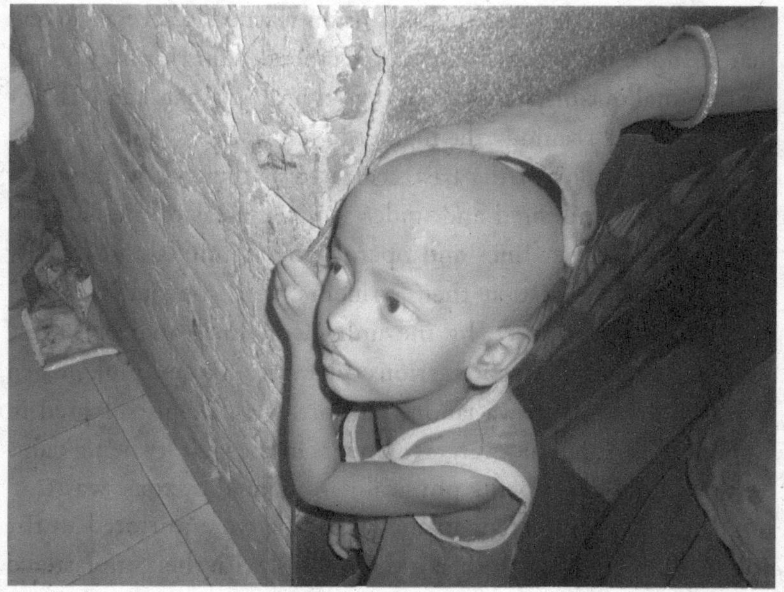

Parveen hit her head badly against a staircase wall during the lockdown. Her distraught mother rushed her to a public hospital which had been turned into a COVID facility. Luckily, there was a doctor willing to stitch up the bleeding toddler.

in a pool of blood." The distraught mother then ran with her baby in her arms looking for an autorickshaw to take her to the nearest public hospital, Madan Mohan Malviya Hospital in South Delhi's Khirki Extension. Despite the skeletal staff assigned to the casualty ward there during the pandemic, Nujita was fortunate enough to reach a doctor who stitched her profusely bleeding daughter up.

Since treating COVID-19 patients was the top-most priority for the public healthcare infrastructure that was stretched to its breaking point during the pandemic, non-COVID patients, many of whom were in need of urgent medical interventions, were left in a lurch. Nivish Gupta, a widower with no children in his mid-40s, lives in a homeless shelter. He used to be a driver, but is now unemployed because of a serious eye condition that has left him unable to see clearly. "I consulted doctors at Aruna Asaf Ali Government

Hospital, Rajpur Road, in Delhi's Civil Lines, and they even fixed my operation schedule. It was at that point that the first lockdown was announced and my operation was postponed," he revealed. When we met him a year and a half later, Nivish had no information about when the operation would take place, which meant that he could also not rejoin duty or get another job as a driver.

Expectant mothers, particularly, were badly hit during this period. Vandana, a community representative of SNS in the Jagdamba Camp area, was in constant touch with residents there during the disturbing spike in COVID-19 infections around the time of the second lockdown in April 2021. Vandana said, "We would phone people and even go from door to door. That was when I came across Meetu (name changed), who lived in Panchsheel Vihar, a neighbourhood adjoining Jagdamba Camp, and learnt that she was pregnant and had contracted Corona. She was in a state of anguish. There was no one she could approach for advice. I asked her whether she had visited a doctor, and she said she had earlier been attending the OPD of a local hospital but because of the *mahamari*, it had been turned into a COVID-19 facility."

Thus began Meetu's desperate hunt for a hospital where she could give birth. The private hospitals were charging exorbitant amounts—something like Rs 17,000 for a normal delivery and three times that amount if it was a caesarean section. The family did not have that kind of money. Meetu's husband was earning half his usual salary and the couple was already deep in debt. In the middle of their search for a hospital bed, they even had to vacate the house they were living in and shift to a smaller premises because the rent had become unaffordable.

Every public hospital in their vicinity claimed that there were no spare beds and the search widened with each passing day. As the due date drew closer, both Meetu and her husband were reduced to a state of panic. Finally, through her husband's Employee's State Insurance Corporation network, they managed a bed in a government hospital in faraway Noida, at the other end of the city. By the

Bearing a child during the pandemic had its share of challenges, from ensuring adequate nutrition for the pregnant woman to accessing a bed in a public hospital.

end of May, the baby was born prematurely and had to be delivered through a caesarean section. Even after this, the struggle continued for Meetu. There were debts to pay and the nutritious food that post-partum mothers like her required was beyond her reach.

Yashoda, of Lal Gumbad basti, also gave birth to a baby girl in June 2020, at a time when family expenses had reached stratospheric heights and earnings had dropped to nil. She was fortunate enough to access a bed in Madan Mohan Malviya Hospital at Khirki, but she had another challenge to face. Because this was her third child, Yashoda was denied the state-provided entitlement of a cash transfer as maternity benefit for supplementing the nutrition of the baby. Yashoda was livid about this, "I cannot understand such a rule—why deprive an innocent baby of a chance for a better life? *Sab bachchon ko milna chahiye* (every child should get these entitlements)." New mothers too stand similarly deprived if they are unable to register or provide the necessary documents.

NFHS data reveals the high levels of anaemia in expectant and post-partum Indian women (Vajpeyi, 2021), and it is very likely that the pandemic has only aggravated this trend. The normal haemoglobin level for a healthy Indian woman should be 12.1 to 15.1 grams per decilitre, (Iron Deficiency Anemia, n.d.), but Jagdamba Camp resident Saleka Begum's reading, when she last took it, was five points. "I feel ill all the time and don't know how long I will last," she sighed. Her biggest challenge is the expense involved, "Even these tests are prohibitive and cost around Rs 4,500 in a private lab. I know that some government hospitals supply iron pills, so if I get them free I am happy. But most often, I end up buying the medicines prescribed to me from the chemist; I don't have the time to stand in queues in a public hospital because I fear I will lose my job if I am late."

The pandemic witnessed cruelties of every kind. Even something as basic as a leave of absence to deal with a serious health crisis at home was denied to Sanjay Rathore, 33, a former clerk at Nigambodh Ghat. We met him in a Yamuna Pushta homeless shelter, where he now lived because he no longer had a job. A father of four, Sanjay had lost his wife to blood cancer nine years ago. Since he had nobody to look after his children, he left them with his father and his father's second wife, who lived some way from Delhi.

After the first lockdown, he received news that his eldest boy, who was 16, had succumbed to an unexplained fever. Said Sanjay,

"I had barely recovered from that, when someone phoned me to say that my younger son, who was 8, had fallen off a ladder—the child died of his injuries a few days later. My whole world was shattered, but I carried on working for the sake of my two daughters. After the second lockdown, when the number of cremations at the ghat had shot up, and bodies were being burnt day and night, I was told that one of my daughters had fallen sick. Going by the earlier tragedies, I was so rattled that I just left my post and ran to look after her. When I came back for duty, I was told that I had been dismissed."

As he related this, Sanjay's face registered a mixture of anger and helplessness. He was full of bitterness over his stepmother's inability to look after the children properly, but most of his ire was directed at his supervisor, "I have worked in Nigambodh Ghat since I was 15. Over 17 years, from performing menial tasks like stacking wood logs, I came to a point where I was given clerical responsibilities. Yet, after all the work I did, I was denied medical leave in a crisis situation." He was now considering approaching the local court over the patent injustice of his dismissal, although the possibility of winning such a case seemed very distant.

The pandemic had exposed major fault lines in the country's healthcare system. Years of neglecting the referral systems linking local communities to primary healthcare centres and sub-centres, and the severe underfunding of government-run medical institutions, had resulted in a public healthcare system that was seriously failing the public. As far back as a year before India's independence, a report of the Bhore Committee had the preamble: "No individual should fail to secure adequate medical care because of inability to pay for it" (Duggal, 1991). Today, those searing words are forgotten. There is a serious lack of social and institutional understanding of what the fundamental right of people to healthcare and well-being should really mean.

Chapter 10

A Mother's Death
in a Summer of Sorrow

By the end of August 2021, after the second wave of the pandemic had receded, the national capital of Delhi counted the number of people it had lost to COVID-19 since April 2020. The toll hovered at a little over 25,000 (Chitre, 2022). This was the official count, but going by the number of "excess deaths" registered by the Civil Registration System, the actual figure could be over 55,000 (Radhakrishnan, 2021).

Each of these deaths spelt the devastation of a family and an abiding grief often marked by feelings of regret and remorse. Could more have been done to prevent that death? This was a question that haunted many in the city, as it did Gautam Giri, living with his wife, Nisha, and baby, Tanvi, in a three-room unit in South Delhi's Savitri Nagar. On a wall in that home is a portrait that signifies the tragedy that has befallen this struggling family. It shows the smiling visage of a woman in her 50s. She was Gautam's mother, Arti Giri, who died of COVID-19 on May 9, 2021.

The story of this mother and son is the archetypal tale of migration for a better life and of finding roots in a big, impersonal metropolis. Gautam related the family history to us, "We came from West Bengal, from the village of Fatehpur, near Digha, about

The smiling portrait of Arti Giri now adorns the wall of her son Gautam's small home. She died of the virus during the pandemic, leaving her son, who had first contracted the disease, inconsolable.

182 km from Kolkata. My father's family owned land, but he died of brain cancer when I was a child of three and a half and his family kept control of his property. The responsibility of supporting the

family now fell entirely on my widowed mother. Her sister took care of me as a child, and it was my mother, working in people's homes in Kolkata, who sent money back home."

When Gautam was a teenager, he came to Delhi with the help of a relative, and began working in a tea shop. His mother joined him. Gautam outlined the trajectory through which their search for work took them, "With papa gone, there was no question of going to school; both my mother and I did casual work to keep going. My mother worked in people's homes, and towards the end of her life, she got a job as a housekeeper in an upmarket locality on a permanent basis. Meanwhile, I did a variety of small jobs, before joining a Gurgaon family as a cook. I worked in that home for ten years."

It seemed as though the tide had turned. For the first time, mother and son had some extra money. Gautam began to develop his driving skills, and decided to trade in his job as a cook for that of a driver—because he preferred to be outdoors rather than shut away in a kitchen. Their world seemed complete when Gautam got married. His wife, Nisha, had worked as a house help in the home where he was employed as a driver.

Nisha broke into our conversation, "Ours was a *prem vivah* (love marriage). My family was opposed to the marriage because we came from different castes, but my mother-in-law was very happy for us. We moved into this home with a rent of Rs 8,000, because of her. She furnished it so that we could live comfortably. *Koi kami nahin thi* (we lacked for nothing). I couldn't have hoped for a better *saas* (mother-in-law)."

Arti was the family's mainstay. She drew a salary of Rs 15,000 a month, and most of that money was spent on her son and his family. When baby Tanvi came, it was the grandmother—whenever she got leave from work—who would pamper her, feed her, bathe her. Gautam reached for the mobile phone to play a video of Arti coaxing Tanvi to eat. "I took this video when she had come home on one of her breaks from work," he explained.

Gautam Giri, with his wife, Nisha, and baby, Tanvi. The family suffered a great deal when both Gautam and his mother fell ill during the second wave. The mother later succumbed to the disease.

The year 2020 changed the easy pace of their life decisively. Gautam, who was working with a taxi service, suddenly found his earnings contract alarmingly. Beside this, there were the added expenses of Nisha's delivery. Gautam remarked, "My income dropped by at least half after the first lockdown was enforced. My mother, who continued to work, helped us immeasurably through it all. Without her assistance, I don't know how we would have survived that year."

But it was the second wave, which began in March–April 2021, that really threw the family into a sea of despair. In mid-April, even as the disease was spreading and beginning to hit large sections of Delhi's population, Gautam began to feel sharp pains in his hands and legs. "I thought it was just fever and took paracetamol, which gave me relief. Every time I felt normal, I would rejoin duty. This carried on for a few days. A point came when I began to find it difficult to breathe. One day, I just collapsed. I don't even remember how I drove, parked the taxi, and came home then. I fell into what was almost a coma outside, by our stairs. A friend helped my wife haul me up to our home. It was clear that there was some *gadbad* (something wrong)." An RT-PCR test conducted on April 20 found him to be COVID-19-positive.

When Arti was informed of this development, she was in total alarm. She immediately sought leave from her employers and came home to look after Gautam. He recalled how she sat with him day and night, pressing his feet, "I was ill and in a daze and was barely able to think clearly, but I remember telling her to wear a mask when she came near me. She didn't take any precautions while tending to me. For her, it was only me and my health that was primary. It was as if she told herself, 'Let him survive, even if I die in the process'."

The 56-year-old woman was in good health until that point, and a test had proved that she was free of the disease. But suddenly, she began to exhibit signs of the virus. She was tested for a second time on April 27. This time there was no ambiguity: the test came back positive. Her daughter-in-law, with the help of a family friend, tried to get her admitted into a hospital. Three big hospitals turned them away. Nisha recalled that nightmare, "The guards at the gate just chased us away rudely, informing us that there were no beds available."

The family had no option but to try and nurse Arti back to health at home. On May 6, they approached a private doctor to come see her at their place. He examined her and felt that there should be no problem. He left behind some medicines. After having the first dose, Arti resisted the treatment, claiming that it only made her feel worse. The doctor had instructed Nisha to procure oxygen, but that was almost impossible at a time when every family of a COVID-19 patient was on the hunt for that lifesaver. The cylinders she managed to get at great expense would be exhausted within 20 minutes. She even approached the local gurudwara, where they had an oxygen *langar* (open community outreach), but they were giving only half a kilo each time, which was barely enough for a few minutes.

Nisha, now nursing two very sick people while handling a toddler, remembered the day Arti died well, "It was May 9. Early in the morning I made *daliya* (porridge of broken wheat). She had no appetite but I coaxed her to eat half a *katori* (small bowl). She then went to sleep. When she woke up a couple of hours later, I could see that she was in great distress. She kept calling out our names. Around 12:30 p.m. that afternoon, she went to the bathroom and collapsed. We desperately called for an ambulance. One turned up but was parked on the outside road, unable to make its way through the narrow lanes of our locality, and no attendant came to our place to take her to the hospital. The ambulance waited a while and then drove off. I was completely helpless. My husband was in no state to do anything. Within half an hour or so, she was dead."

The death certificate that was issued by the South Delhi Municipal Corporation noted that she had died at home.

It was only through his mother's well-placed employers that Gautam was able to manage a slot to cremate her body at the Ganga Vihar electric crematorium at Sarai Kale Khan—in another far corner of the city. "In our custom, we usually bathe the body before cremation, but we could not do this. Call it a miracle if you want, but that evening, the skies opened up and my mother's body was bathed in rain water. The scenes at the crematorium were devastating. Lines of people were waiting to cremate the bodies of their loved ones, and half-burnt bodies were being discarded because the crematorium had run out of fuel," remembered Gautam. Just thinking of that day clouded his normally affable expression, "*Zindagi asaan nahin hain, maut bhi asaan nahin hain* (life is not easy, neither is death)."

He could complete his mother's funeral arrangements only with the greatest of difficulty. It took him a long time to recover from his illness and the emotionally draining experience of losing her, "For one and a half months, I was in such a condition that people looking at me would say that I looked like a burnt body." What filled him with regret even three months after Arti's demise, was the fact that his mother's love for him was so blind that she did not take care of her own life. Said the son, "All her life, she struggled. Once

Gautam plays a video of his late mother, Arti, feeding his baby in better times. "The only thing she wanted was a better life for us," he says.

her husband died, his family captured the property that should have come to her. She was fiercely driven by the wish to ensure that I could have a better life than she did." He played the video again, showing Arti in happier times feeding her granddaughter, and a smile formed around his lips. "Such a doting grandmother she was. How she loved Tanvi!"

News of Arti's death by COVID-19 reached the highest levels of the state government, and Gautam even received a standardised letter of condolence from the Chief Minister of Delhi, Arvind Kejriwal, which was full of comforting words. All the medical and funeral expenses, and loss of livelihood due to Gautam's illness had meant that the family now faced a debt of around Rs 2 lakh. Recovering from his bout with the disease had left him physically weaker, "Even now, I get breathless while climbing the stairs. Anxiety and regret keep me awake; I get only a few hours of sleep at night. I am now working hard as a driver for one family, earning about Rs 16,000 a month," he revealed.

It was tough to save enough from this amount to repay the money owed, with half the salary going towards rent. There was also a commitment to send Rs 500 to Arti's mother, back in the village. What particularly distressed the young couple were calls from those to whom they owed money. These calls were now coming in thick and fast. Every time it happened, Gautam felt a rush of anxiety and helplessness, "I would like to clear my dues quickly, but that's just not possible."

On June 24, the Delhi government notified its COVID-19 death compensation policy, which provided an ex gratia sum of Rs 50,000 to the next of kin of those who lost their lives to COVID-19. It required documents like proof of residence of both the deceased and the next of kin; a death certificate; certification that the death was due to COVID-19, or one that took place within a month of testing positive and verified by the health department as a COVID death; as well as documents establishing the relationship between the applicant and the deceased.

Gautam had all the documentation and filed his application, "We desperately needed that compensation—it will help us settle at least a part of our outstandings," he said. He didn't hear anything about it from the authorities for a long while, and he worried that some loophole would be cited to deny him the money. According to news reports, there were several hundreds of people like him waiting for their dues—in some cases, even after their requests had been verified. After the SNS assisted Gautam in filing an RTI query to find out the status of his application, things started to move along, and Gautam was assured by the authorities that he would get the compensation. After months of unceasing worry, the much-needed relief came in.

The times continue to be extremely uncertain for the young family. The only thing Gautam was sure of was that no amount of money could compensate for the loss of a woman who had struggled all her life to ensure that her son got a foothold in life—and did so, right to her last breath.

Afterword

Collective Struggle Inspires Hope Amidst Crisis

Anjali Bhardwaj and Amrita Johri

The national lockdown imposed in India on March 25, 2020, led to acute distress for hundreds of thousands in the informal sector, many of whom were migrant workers. One of the harshest lockdowns globally was announced by Prime Minister Narendra Modi with a four-hour notice.

The directive to "work from home" was a classic testament to the gaping abyss between the lived realities of millions, and government planning. How could a street hawker selling *chhole bhature* (chick pea and leavened bread) from his food cart, or a woman working as domestic help, work from home? The announcement of the lockdown was not accompanied with the roll out of requisite emergency relief to deal with the crisis caused by the cessation of income-generating activities. No thought was put into how 90 per cent of the workforce which is in the informal sector, including daily wagers and self-employed workers with no social security and income security to fall back on, would manage to pay rent or even purchase food for their families.

With no resources to sustain themselves and no public transport, lakhs of migrant workers started the journey back home on foot. Those left behind struggled to prepare two meals a day and risked being evicted from their homes. Thousands of informal sector workers who lived a hand-to-mouth existence in *jhuggis* thronged to the night shelters on account of being unable to pay rent, only to be turned away as the demand far outstripped provisions made by the government.

As the unprecedented humanitarian crisis unfolded, SNS and other civil society groups across Delhi received thousands of SOS calls for food, especially from those who did not possess ration cards and were left out of the ambit of the National Food Security Act. The most marginalised— migrant workers, families living on rent in bastis, homeless persons—were mostly excluded from the food security net due to their inability to furnish the myriad documents necessary to procure a card, like Aadhaar numbers, copies of their electricity bill with their residential address and a declaration that the annual family income was less than Rs 1,00,000. Those living in bastis on rent had no formal tenancy agreements which could be used as proof of address. For the homeless population, the possibility of obtaining a ration card was next to impossible. The income limit of Rs 8,000 per month was completely impractical, given that the rent for a single room in the basti was nearly Rs 3,000. Even the government's poverty line was completely out of sync with reality.

In response to the crisis, the Delhi Rozi Roti Adhikar Abhiyan (DRRAA), a network of individuals and organisations in Delhi working over the last 10 years to mobilise communities and to engage with governments to ensure right to food for all, raised direct support to provide rations. DRRAA also took up the issue with the state government, and wrote to the Chief Minister of Delhi, highlighting the need for emergency measures required to ensure access to food and to prevent starvation deaths during the COVID-19 crisis. DRRAA urged the government to provide cooked food for those in need through anganwadis and government schools, expand the food bracket for ration card holders by including cooking oil and pulses and, most importantly, universalise the Public

Distribution System (PDS) by providing rations to all persons in need of food security, irrespective of whether or not they possessed a ration card.

On April 1, 2020, the Delhi government announced that it would provide dry rations through e-coupons as a one-time relief measure to ten lakh people who did not possess ration cards. Ironically, however, the scheme that was meant for the welfare of the poorest required that the application be made only in online mode. A letter sent by DRRAA on April 7, 2020, highlighted the exclusionary procedure:

> The system requires those without ration cards to apply for an e-coupon using a website to register themselves for accessing rations. They need to have the ability to access the internet, have a mobile phone to generate an OTP, upload a photo of their aadhaar card and a photo of their family, and finally, download the e-coupon. …**In the current emergency situation,** an elaborate system…**will make rations inaccessible to the poorest and most marginalized who need it the most**.

At a time when ration distribution by the government—both through ration cards and through e-coupons—became a lifeline for the vast majority of the population, SNS and other constituent members of DRRAA realised the urgent need and importance of peoples' monitoring of the ration distribution system to ensure that the relief actually reaches the beneficiaries.

To monitor the distribution of foodgrain and document the challenges faced by people in accessing rations through ration cards and e-coupons, DRRAA volunteers across Delhi started visiting the distribution points and ration shops to undertake social audits. The social audit reports highlighted several concerns, including delay in ration distribution, and the problem of shops being shut during working hours, which forced people to make multiple visits to procure their entitlements.

As the distress among people became dire, and relief efforts by the government continued to be patchy at best, DRRAA filed a petition in its ongoing public interest litigation, highlighting the need to universalise ration distribution to include all those in need and to ensure effective redress of complaints of non-supply of rations. The matter was heard by the Delhi High Court on April 27, 2020, and the Court gave landmark directions to ensure food security for all. The High Court directed that rations must be provided to everyone in need, irrespective of whether or not they possessed a ration card. Dismissing the government's contention that universal distribution of foodgrain would mean that even those not in need would avail of this benefit, the bench observed that during a pandemic, only those in dire need would stand in queues at ration shops for five kg of grain. The court later also ordered the setting up of help-desks in all schools from where rations were being provided for those without ration cards, to assist people in navigating the online system of e-coupons.

The directions provided much needed relief; they helped to ensure that lakhs of people got food security at the peak of the crisis. Following the orders of the Delhi High Court in the DRRAA case, 69.6 lakh persons who did not possess ration cards registered under the e-coupon scheme and were provided rations. This number showed the large-scale exclusion of the needy from the food security net: out of a population of around 1.9 crore in Delhi, 72 lakh possessed ration cards, and another 70 lakh required rations from the government to sustain themselves during the crisis.

In the interim, following criticism over the mishandling of the migrant workers' crisis, the central government also announced the Atmanirbhar Bharat Yojana, under which 8 crore migrant workers in the country, who did not possess ration cards, were to be provided 5 kg of rations per person for two months.

Distribution of rations to those without ration cards was unfortunately stopped after two months by the state government, citing the formal lifting of the lockdown, even though people continued to face economic distress.

As the second wave of COVID-19 hit the country the following year, the Delhi government imposed another lockdown for nearly six weeks in the months of April and May 2021. This led to the condition of the urban poor becoming even more precarious. Having exhausted their meagre savings in coping with the 2020 lockdown, they had nothing to cushion their distress when work stopped in 2021. In addition, many families also faced the brunt of the virus. In a bid to save their loved ones, they were forced to shell out exorbitant amounts for oxygen and essential medicines which were being sold in the black market due to extreme shortages and poor healthcare delivery. The second wave became a debt trap for many in the city who took loans to survive the twin crisis of economic distress and health.

Despite the exacerbated and visible distress during the second wave, no relief programme to ensure food security was announced, while at the same time restrictions were placed on economic activity. DRRAA wrote to the government, urging it to immediately restart the scheme for providing rations to those without ration cards by universalising the public distribution system, and suggested the issuance of temporary COVID ration cards to distribute rations on a monthly basis as long as the COVID-19 pandemic lasted. Three activists also petitioned the Supreme Court in the suo motu case regarding the distress faced by migrant workers across the country, urging the apex court to hear the matter and intervene to direct provision of basic food and social security. On May 13, 2021, the SC directed that all migrant workers in Delhi NCR be provided rations and cooked food. Taking into cognisance exclusions on account of the inability to furnish necessary documents, the Court directed that self-certification for establishing identity be allowed.

Finally, at a press conference on May 18, 2021, the Delhi government announced that they will put in place a scheme to provide rations to those not covered under the PDS. When, more than a week later, there was still no sign of the policy being implemented, DRRAA highlighted the inordinate delay in a letter to the government:

> This is most concerning as distress among the working poor and marginalised communities is alarmingly high as Delhi is now in the SIXTH week of the lockdown. This delay is forcing people to rely on private charities and neighbours for food and in many places people are being forced to beg for food. The continuous extensions of the lockdown with no food relief for those without ration cards is inhuman. It is an indication of the desperate situation people are in that the joint food relief initiative which DRRAA and other groups are part of, has received SOS requests for ration from 1.50 lakh people across Delhi. Most of these are people without ration cards.

On May 28, when the Delhi government finally notified the guidelines, it only provided for a one-time relief of five kg of rations with a pre-determined cap of 20 lakh people, even though 70 lakh people had availed of benefits under a similar scheme during the first wave. Reports by DRRAA based on visits to distribution centres documented the intense crisis, including the impact of the government placing unofficial curbs on providing rations by restricting distribution to only 60–100 families in a day per school which had led to people queuing up from 3:00 a.m. in the morning. Fights erupted outside many distribution centres indicating the desperation of people. Utterly inadequate provisioning led to the closure of several centres which had signboards outside announcing '*ration khatam hai*' (ration has finished), forcing people to return home empty-handed.

In a hearing of the DRRAA matter in June 2021, the Delhi High Court observed that a cap of 20 lakh persons "is a substantial underestimate" and "is an exercise in arbitrariness since that number appears to be improvised". It further noted that it was "not sure if styling the food relief exercise as a 'one-time measure' would subserve the purpose of the policy". The Delhi government counsel assured the Court that the Delhi Cabinet was seized of the matter of reviewing the policy decision. In its order, the Court noted, "We accordingly await the decision of the Delhi Cabinet appropriately revising the number of Non-PDS beneficiaries under the scheme in question." The revised policy never came and distribution dwindled as stocks were not replenished.

The struggle to ensure food security continues. The latest affidavit filed by the Delhi government before the High Court claimed that it had done away with the restriction of one-time distribution and increased the cap to 30 lakh persons, but the distribution on the ground remained at a virtual stand-still, with most distribution centres having no stocks. Of the 54 schools audited by DRRAA in the third week of September 2021, 53 had no stocks and were not distributing any rations.

Even as the struggle for food and social security during the COVID-19 crisis continues, the larger task of re-imagining and building a socio-economic framework, where the contribution of unorganised sector workers is properly recognised and valued, carries on.

Bibliography

2020. "Mental Health in the times of COVID-19 Pandemic ." Department of Psychiatry, National Institute of Mental Health & Neurosciences.

Anand, Ishan, and Anjana Thampi. 2020. Less than a third of Indians go to public hospitals for treatment. *Mint*. May 4.

Bakhla, Nirali, Jean Dreze, Reetika Khera, and Vipul Paikra. 2021. Locked out: Emergency report on school education. *Frontline*. October 8.

Bhardwaj, Deeksha. 2021. Over 1.3 million migrants left Delhi during 2nd wave of Covid-19, shows data. *The Hindustan Times*. July 2.

Bose, Shritama. 2021. Manappuram Finance auctions Rs 404 crore worth gold in Jan-March quarter. *Money Control*. May 26.

Burman, Sourav Roy. 2021. Senior citizens, differently-abled in Delhi can designate nominees to collect ration. *The Indian Express*. August 30.

Chaudhry, Shivani, Deepak Kumar, Anagha Jaipal, Aishwarya Ayushmaan, Dev Pal, and Shanta Devi. 2021. Forced evictions in India in 2020: A grave human rights crisis during the pandemic. Housing and Land Rights Network.

Chettri, Shradha. 2021. 1.6 lakh Delhi students move from private to government schools. *The Times of India*. September 14.

Cleveland Clinic. n.d. Alcohol use disorder. https://my.clevelandclinic.org/health/diseases/3909-alcoholism.

Cunningham, Alison, and Linda Baker. n.d. Little eyes, little ears...how violence against a mother shapes children as they grow. The Centre for Children and Families in the Justice System.

Dalberg Advisors. 2021. The Disproportionate impact of Covid-19 on women in India—and new hope for recovery efforts. August.

Deshpande, Ashwini, and Rajesh Ramachandran. 2020. Which Indian children are short and why? social identity, childhood malnutrition and cognitive outcomes. Economics Discussion Papers. Ashoka University, March 2.

Dhingra, Swati, and Maitreesh Ghatak. 2021. How has Covid-19 affected India's economy? Economics Observatory. June 30.

Duggal, Ravi. 1991. Bhore Committee (1946) and its relevance today. *The Indian Journal of Pediatrics* 58: 395–406.

Gile, Maggie. 2021. India's cost of COVID ICU care treatment equals 16 months of pay for day laborers. *Newsweek*. July 26.

Government of India. n.d. PRAGYATA guidelines for digital education. Department of School Education & Literacy Ministry of Human Resource Development, Government of India.

HelpAge India. 2020. Impact and challenges faced by elders in time of Covid-19, HelpAge India. July 17.

HT Correspondent. 2007. Rang de basti. *The Hindustan Times*. May 7.

Huxhold, Oliver, Elena Hees, and Noah J. Webster. 2020. Towards bridging the grey digital divide: changes in internet access and its predictors from 2002 to 2014 in Germany. *European Journal of Ageing* 17: 271–280.

IANS. 2020. Tablighi super spreaders cause Covid-19 explosion in India. *The Times of India*. April 2.

ILO, UNICEF. 2020. COVID-19 and child labour - A time of crisis, a time to act.

Jagori. 2020. Impact of COVID-19 and the lockdowns on women in select communities of Delhi.

Jejeebhoy, Shireen. 2021. Child marriages during the pandemic. *The India Forum*. June 14.

Mander, Harsh. 2020. *Locking down the poor: The pandemic and India's moral centre*. Speaking Tiger.

Mondal, Dipak. 2020. Tax on alcohol: More states to follow Delhi's 70% special Corona fee on liquor. *Business Today*. May 5.

N. Neetha. 2021. Crisis After crisis: The pandemic and women's work, Volume: 69. *The Indian Economic Journal* 69 (3).

n.d. Iron deficiency anemia. National Health Portal of India. http://nhp. gov.in/disease/blood-lymphatic/iron-deficiency-anemia#:~:text=Normal%20Hemoglobin%20Levels%3A%20Hemoglobin%20is,12.1%20to%2015.1%20gm%2Fdl.

n.d. World Elder Abuse Awareness Day, 15th June, 2021, Human rights of elderly are at stake. Agewell.

National Institute of Urban Affairs. n.d. Baseline report shelter-MPD 2041 as an enabling strategic plan.

News18. 2021. NCRB data shows 50% rise in child marriage cases in 2020; Experts say more reporting may be factor. *News18*. September 18.

Pradhan, Bibhudatta, Upmanyu Trivedi, and Bloomberg. 2020. Coronavirus: Delhi's Nizamuddin, Noida among 10 latest COVID-19 hotspots in India. *Mint*. March 31.

PTI. 2021. Closure of 1.5 million schools due to COVID-19 impacted 247 million children in India: UNICEF study. *The Times of India*. March 4.

Special Correspondent. 2020. "Special Corona fee" on liquor in Delhi. *The Hindu*. May 5.

Srivastava, Prashansa, and Prachi Shukla. 2021. Crisis behind doors: Domestic workers' struggles during the pandemic and beyond." *Economic & Political Weekly*.

Staff Reporter. 2020. 13 out of 37 ration shops found closed: DRAA report, *The Hindu*. April 10.

United Nations Human Rights Office of the High Commissioner. n.d. Protecting the right to housing in the context of the COVID-19 outbreak, Special Rapporteur on the right to adequate housing. United Nations Human Rights Office of the High Commissioner.

Vajpeyi, Alok. 2021. NFHS-5 Data shows Anaemia among women and children is on the rise. *The Quint*. November 29.

Verderosa, Dan. 2021. Indian women's nutrition suffered during COVID-19 lockdown, Tata-Cornell Study, Tata-Cornell Institute for Agriculture and Nutrition. July 27.

About the Authors

Pamela Philipose is at present the ombudsperson of *The Wire.in*. She has been director and editor-in-chief of Women's Feature Service, a features agency mandated to visibilise gender in media coverage, and earlier she was senior associate editor with *The Indian Express*, anchoring the edit and op-ed pages. She has been awarded the Chameli Devi Jain Award for Outstanding Woman Journalist and was given the Zee-Asthiva award for her journalism. Her book, *Media's Shifting Terrain Five Years that Transformed the Way India Communicates,* was published by Orient BlackSwan in 2019.

Anjali Bhardwaj is the founder of Satark Nagrik Sangathan (SNS), a citizens' group working in the slum settlements of Delhi, with a mandate to promote transparency and accountability in government functioning. SNS works closely with marginalised communities on issues of food and social security. She has been associated with the Right to Information (RTI) movement in India for over two decades and is a co-convenor of the National Campaign for Peoples' Right to Information (NCPRI). She is a member of the Steering Committee of the National Right to Food Campaign and the Delhi Rozi Roti Adhikar Abhiyan.

Amrita Johri leads the information and research initiatives at Satark Nagrik Sangathan (SNS). She is a member of the working committee of the National Campaign for Peoples' Right to Information (NCPRI) and is part of the convening group of the National Right to Food Campaign and Delhi Rozi Roti Adhikar Abhiyan (Delhi Right to Food Campaign).

9 789382 579885